ALGORITHMS

COMPUTER SCIENCE UNVEILED

4 BOOKS IN 1

BOOK 1
COMPUTER SCIENCE: ALGORITHMS UNVEILED

BOOK 2
MASTERING ALGORITHMS: FROM BASICS TO EXPERT LEVEL

BOOK 3
ALGORITHMIC MASTERY: A JOURNEY FROM NOVICE TO GURU

BOOK 4
ALGORITHMIC WIZARDRY: UNRAVELING COMPLEXITY FOR EXPERTS

ROB BOTWRIGHT

Published by Rob Botwright
Library of Congress Cataloging-in-Publication Data
ISBN 978-1-83938-620-6
Cover design by Rizzo

Disclaimer

The contents of this book are based on extensive research and the best available historical sources. However, the author and publisher make no claims, promises, or guarantees about the accuracy, completeness, or adequacy of the information contained herein. The information in this book is provided on an "as is" basis, and the author and publisher disclaim any and all liability for any errors, omissions, or inaccuracies in the information or for any actions taken in reliance on such information. The opinions and views expressed in this book are those of the author and do not necessarily reflect the official policy or position of any organization or individual mentioned in this book. Any reference to specific people, places, or events is intended only to provide historical context and is not intended to defame or malign any group, individual, or entity. The information in this book is intended for educational and entertainment purposes only. It is not intended to be a substitute for professional advice or judgment. Readers are encouraged to conduct their own research and to seek professional advice where appropriate. Every effort has been made to obtain necessary permissions and acknowledgments for all images and other copyrighted material used in this book. Any errors or omissions in this regard are unintentional, and the author and publisher will correct them in future editions.

BOOK 1 - COMPUTER SCIENCE: ALGORITHMS UNVEILED

BOOK 2 - MASTERING ALGORITHMS: FROM BASICS TO EXPERT LEVEL

BOOK 3 - ALGORITHMIC MASTERY: A JOURNEY FROM NOVICE TO GURU

BOOK 4 - ALGORITHMIC WIZARDRY: UNRAVELING COMPLEXITY FOR EXPERTS

Introduction

Welcome to the world of algorithms—a universe where logic, creativity, and computational wizardry converge to unlock the mysteries of computer science. In this captivating book bundle titled "ALGORITHMS: COMPUTER SCIENCE UNVEILED," we invite you to embark on an illuminating journey through the heart of computer science and algorithmic mastery. Across four meticulously crafted volumes, we will unravel the intricate tapestry of algorithms, from their fundamental concepts to the realms of expert-level complexity.

"BOOK 1 - COMPUTER SCIENCE: ALGORITHMS UNVEILED" serves as your entry point into this exciting voyage. Within its pages, you will discover the foundational principles that underpin the world of algorithms. Whether you're a newcomer to computer science or an experienced enthusiast, this volume will equip you with the essential building blocks required to navigate the world of algorithms.

As we progress, "BOOK 2 - MASTERING ALGORITHMS: FROM BASICS TO EXPERT LEVEL" will elevate your understanding to new heights. We will delve into the depths of algorithmic thinking, explore advanced sorting and searching techniques, and uncover the power of dynamic programming and greedy algorithms. With each chapter, you will ascend the ladder of algorithmic proficiency, culminating in the expertise needed to tackle complex computational challenges.

"BOOK 3 - ALGORITHMIC MASTERY: A JOURNEY FROM NOVICE TO GURU" is designed to nurture your growth from novice to guru. This volume will immerse you in the world of divide and conquer strategies, introduce you to advanced data structures and their applications, and present you with algorithmic challenges that demand a mastery of the art. It's a transformative journey that will test your mettle and hone your problem-solving abilities.

Finally, in "BOOK 4 - ALGORITHMIC WIZARDRY: UNRAVELING COMPLEXITY FOR EXPERTS," we will push the boundaries of your algorithmic expertise. Here, you will explore expert-level techniques, conquer algorithmic puzzles and enigmas, and unleash the full power of your algorithmic mastery. This volume is for those who aspire to become true wizards in the field, capable of navigating the most intricate computational landscapes.

Whether you are a student, a professional, or simply someone with an insatiable curiosity about the inner workings of computer science, "ALGORITHMS: COMPUTER SCIENCE UNVEILED" has something to offer. It is a comprehensive resource that spans the entire spectrum of algorithmic knowledge, catering to beginners and experts alike.

Join us on this enlightening journey through the captivating world of algorithms—a world where logic meets creativity, and where problem-solving knows no bounds. As we embark on this adventure together, prepare to unveil the secrets of computer science, master the art of algorithmic thinking, and ultimately, become an algorithmic wizard in your own right.

BOOK 1
COMPUTER SCIENCE
ALGORITHMS UNVEILED

ROB BOTWRIGHT

Chapter 1: The Building Blocks of Algorithms

In the world of computer science, understanding the fundamentals of algorithms is essential for any aspiring programmer or developer. Algorithms are the step-by-step procedures that computers follow to solve problems and perform tasks. They are the heart and soul of computer programs, and mastering them is a crucial skill for anyone in the field of computer science. Next, we will embark on a journey to explore the algorithmic foundations that form the basis of all computational processes.

At its core, an algorithm is a set of well-defined instructions that take some input, process it, and produce an output. These instructions are like the building blocks of software, enabling computers to perform tasks ranging from simple calculations to complex data analysis. Whether you're designing a new app, optimizing a website, or solving intricate mathematical problems, algorithms play a central role in achieving your goals.

To appreciate the significance of algorithms, one must recognize their ubiquity in our modern lives. From search engines that help us find information on the internet to navigation systems guiding us to our destinations, algorithms are behind the scenes, working tirelessly to make our digital experiences seamless and efficient. Moreover, algorithms are used in a wide range of fields, from healthcare and finance to artificial intelligence and robotics.

One of the key aspects of algorithms is their ability to be represented in various forms, including pseudocode, flowcharts, and programming languages. These representations allow developers to communicate their ideas effectively and implement algorithms in different programming environments. By understanding how to express algorithms in these forms, you'll gain a versatile skill set that can be applied to a wide array of programming languages and platforms.

In addition to their practical applications, algorithms have a rich history dating back to ancient civilizations. The word "algorithm" itself is derived from the name of the Persian mathematician and scholar, Muhammad ibn Musa al-Khwarizmi, who lived in the 9th century. Al-Khwarizmi made significant contributions to mathematics and introduced the concept of algebra, which is rooted in algorithmic problem-solving.

As we delve deeper into this chapter, we'll explore the fundamental characteristics of algorithms, such as determinism and finiteness. Determinism means that given the same input, an algorithm will always produce the same output, ensuring reliability and predictability. Finiteness implies that an algorithm must have a clear endpoint, meaning it will eventually terminate and produce an output.

Furthermore, algorithms can be categorized based on their purpose and behavior. Some algorithms are designed to search for specific items in a dataset, while others aim to sort data in a specific order. Optimization algorithms seek the best solution among many possibilities, making them valuable in fields like operations research and machine learning.

Throughout this book, we will encounter algorithms from various categories, each with its unique characteristics and applications. You will learn how to analyze algorithmic efficiency, which is crucial for making informed decisions when selecting algorithms for different tasks. This knowledge will empower you to choose the most suitable algorithm for a given problem, taking into account factors like time complexity and space complexity.

As we proceed, we will also discuss algorithmic design paradigms, such as divide and conquer, dynamic programming, and greedy algorithms. These paradigms provide structured approaches to solving complex problems by breaking them down into smaller, more manageable subproblems. Understanding these paradigms will enhance your problem-solving skills and equip you with powerful tools for tackling a wide range of challenges.

In summary, this chapter serves as the foundation upon which your journey into the world of algorithms will be built. We have explored the essential concepts and historical significance of algorithms, setting the stage for a comprehensive exploration of algorithmic techniques and strategies in the subsequent chapters. As you continue reading, remember that mastering algorithms is not just about learning rules; it's about developing a problem-solving mindset and the ability to craft elegant solutions to real-world problems. So, let's embark on this algorithmic journey together, discovering the beauty and power of algorithms in computer science.

Algorithm design principles form the cornerstone of creating efficient and effective algorithms. These principles are the guiding rules that help programmers and computer scientists craft algorithms that solve complex problems while optimizing for time and space efficiency.

At the heart of algorithm design lies the concept of abstraction, which involves simplifying complex problems into manageable components that can be solved step by step. Abstraction allows developers to focus on high-level concepts without getting bogged down in the details of implementation.

When designing algorithms, it's essential to begin with a clear problem statement, defining the input, output, and the specific requirements that the algorithm must meet. This step ensures that the algorithm's objectives are well-defined and align with the problem it aims to solve.

A fundamental principle in algorithm design is breaking down a problem into smaller, more manageable subproblems. This divide-and-conquer approach simplifies complex tasks by solving each subproblem separately and then combining their solutions to obtain the overall result.

Recursive algorithms, which call themselves with smaller instances of the same problem, are a powerful tool in divide-and-conquer strategies. They allow for elegant solutions to problems that exhibit a recursive structure.

Efficient algorithms optimize for time complexity, which measures the algorithm's running time as a function of the input size. Algorithms with lower time complexity are preferable because they can handle larger datasets and provide faster results.

Space complexity, another critical aspect of algorithm design, evaluates the algorithm's memory usage. Algorithms with lower space complexity use less memory and are often more efficient, especially in resource-constrained environments.

One crucial principle to consider is algorithmic correctness. An algorithm must produce the correct output for all valid inputs while adhering to the defined requirements. Ensuring correctness involves rigorous testing and validation procedures.

When dealing with large datasets or complex problems, algorithmic efficiency becomes paramount. Efficiency often involves making trade-offs between time and space complexity, balancing the algorithm's performance with its resource utilization.

Greedy algorithms are a class of algorithms that make locally optimal choices at each step, hoping to find a globally optimal solution. These algorithms are particularly useful in problems where making the best choice at each step leads to an optimal overall solution.

Dynamic programming, on the other hand, breaks a problem into overlapping subproblems and stores their solutions to avoid redundant computations. This technique is especially valuable for optimization problems.

In algorithm design, heuristic approaches are often employed when an optimal solution is hard to find. Heuristics are rules of thumb that guide the algorithm towards a satisfactory solution, even if it may not be the absolute best.

Algorithms may need to handle special cases or edge cases, which are inputs or situations that differ from the norm. Considering these cases and designing algorithms to handle them gracefully is an essential design principle.

An algorithm's design should also account for scalability, as it may need to process larger datasets or handle increased workloads over time. Scalable algorithms can adapt to changing requirements and growing input sizes.

Parallelism is a design principle that leverages multiple processing units to execute tasks simultaneously, increasing the algorithm's speed and efficiency. Parallel algorithms are critical in the era of multi-core processors and distributed computing.

Another crucial aspect of algorithm design is robustness, which ensures that an algorithm performs reliably even in the presence of unexpected or erroneous inputs. Robust algorithms gracefully handle errors and exceptions.

Security considerations should not be overlooked in algorithm design, especially when handling sensitive data. Designing algorithms with security in mind helps protect against vulnerabilities and potential threats.

Algorithms may also need to be adaptable and customizable, allowing users to fine-tune their behavior according to specific requirements. Providing configurable parameters and options enhances an algorithm's flexibility.

Documentation is an often underestimated but crucial part of algorithm design. Well-documented algorithms are easier for others to understand, maintain, and extend. Clear comments and explanations within the code are essential.

In practice, algorithm design often involves a process of iteration and refinement. Initial designs may undergo multiple revisions to improve efficiency, correctness, and robustness.

Collaboration and code review with peers can be valuable during algorithm design. Different perspectives and insights can lead to better-designed algorithms and catch potential issues early.

Real-world testing and benchmarking are essential steps in algorithm design. Evaluating an algorithm's performance on actual data provides valuable insights into its strengths and weaknesses.

Algorithm design is not a one-size-fits-all endeavor. The choice of algorithmic approach depends on the specific problem at hand, the available resources, and the desired trade-offs between various factors.

As we delve deeper into the world of algorithm design principles, we will explore real-world examples and case studies that illustrate these principles in action. By understanding and applying these principles, you'll be equipped to create efficient, robust, and scalable algorithms that solve complex problems in the field of computer science and beyond.

In summary, algorithm design principles are the guiding rules and strategies that enable developers and computer scientists to create algorithms that efficiently solve problems, meet requirements, and adapt to various scenarios. These principles encompass a wide range of considerations, from abstraction and correctness to efficiency, scalability, and security. By mastering these principles, you'll be well-prepared to tackle challenging algorithmic tasks and contribute to the advancement of computer science and technology.

Chapter 2: Understanding Algorithmic Complexity

In the realm of algorithm analysis and design, understanding Big O notation and time complexity is paramount. Big O notation is a mathematical notation used to describe the upper bound or worst-case performance of an algorithm in terms of the input size. It provides a standardized way to express how the runtime of an algorithm grows relative to the size of the input. The 'O' in Big O stands for "order of" and is followed by a mathematical function that represents the upper bound on the algorithm's execution time. For example, if an algorithm's runtime is described as $O(n)$, it means that the algorithm's execution time grows linearly with the size of the input (n). In other words, if the input size doubles, the algorithm's runtime will also double. Big O notation is a valuable tool for comparing and analyzing algorithms because it allows us to abstract away constant factors and lower-order terms. This abstraction helps us focus on the fundamental relationship between input size and runtime. To illustrate this, consider two algorithms: one with a runtime of 5n and another with a runtime of $2n^2$. Although the first algorithm has a lower coefficient, the second algorithm has a higher order term, and its runtime will eventually surpass the first algorithm's as the input size grows. Big O notation provides a concise way to express this comparison by stating that the first algorithm is $O(n)$, and the second algorithm is $O(n^2)$. Common Big O notations include $O(1)$ for constant time algorithms, $O(\log n)$ for logarithmic time algorithms, $O(n)$ for linear time algorithms, $O(n \log n)$ for linearithmic time algorithms, $O(n^2)$ for quadratic time algorithms, and $O(2^n)$ for exponential time algorithms. Understanding these notations allows you to assess the efficiency of algorithms and choose the most appropriate one for a given problem. When analyzing the time complexity of an algorithm, it's essential to focus on the worst-case scenario. The worst-case scenario represents the situation in which the algorithm takes the longest time to complete, ensuring that your algorithm performs adequately under all circumstances. While the average-case and best-case analyses can provide valuable insights, they may not account for situations where the algorithm faces the most significant challenges. For example, in a sorting algorithm, the worst-case scenario might involve sorting an already sorted list in descending order, which requires more time than sorting an unsorted list. By considering the worst-case time complexity, you can make informed decisions about algorithm selection, especially when dealing with critical applications or large datasets. Analyzing the time complexity of an algorithm typically involves examining its control flow, loops, and recursive calls. Each step in the algorithm contributes to its overall runtime, and understanding how these steps scale with input size is essential for determining its Big O notation. In some cases, the time complexity of an algorithm may depend on multiple factors, such as the number of nested loops or conditional branches. In such cases, you can express the overall time complexity as a combination of these factors, simplifying it to the dominant term when identifying the Big O notation. Consider a searching algorithm that iterates through a two-dimensional array using nested loops. The time complexity of this algorithm may be expressed as $O(m * n)$, where m is the number of rows and n is the number of columns in the array. When analyzing recursive algorithms, you should consider the number of recursive calls and the work done in each call. For example, a recursive algorithm that divides the input size by two in each call and performs a constant amount of work would have a time complexity of O(log n). However, a recursive algorithm that divides the input size by a constant factor greater than two and performs linear work in each call would have a time complexity of O(n). In addition to time complexity, it's crucial to assess space complexity, which measures the amount of memory an algorithm requires relative to the input size. Space complexity is also expressed using Big O notation, with common notations like O(1) for constant space, O(log n) for logarithmic space, O(n) for linear space, and O(n^2) for quadratic space. Analyzing space complexity is essential when dealing with limited memory resources or when optimizing algorithms for memory-efficient execution. For example, algorithms that use recursion may consume additional memory on the call stack, potentially leading to higher space complexity. To optimize algorithms for space efficiency, you may need to explore iterative solutions or dynamic programming techniques that minimize memory usage. In practical algorithm design, achieving a balance between time complexity and space complexity is often necessary. An algorithm with lower time complexity may use more memory, while an algorithm optimized for space may require additional computational time. The choice between these trade-offs depends on the specific requirements and constraints of the problem you are solving. To summarize, Big O notation and time complexity analysis are fundamental tools for evaluating the efficiency of algorithms. Understanding these concepts allows you to make informed decisions when selecting and designing algorithms for various computational tasks. By focusing on the worst-case scenario and considering both time and space complexity, you can develop algorithms that perform optimally and meet the demands of real-world applications.

In the realm of algorithm analysis and design, space complexity and memory usage are crucial considerations that go hand in hand with time complexity. While time complexity measures how efficiently an algorithm performs in terms of execution time, space complexity evaluates how efficiently it utilizes memory. Understanding and optimizing space complexity is essential, especially in scenarios with limited memory resources, such as embedded systems, mobile devices, or cloud computing environments.

Space complexity, expressed using Big O notation, quantifies the amount of memory an algorithm requires relative to the size of its input. Common space complexities include $O(1)$ for constant space, $O(\log n)$ for logarithmic space, $O(n)$ for linear space, and $O(n^2)$ for quadratic space. These notations provide a standardized way to communicate how an algorithm's memory usage scales with input size.

Constant space complexity, denoted as $O(1)$, means that an algorithm uses a fixed amount of memory, regardless of the input size. This is typically achieved by declaring a fixed number of variables or data structures that do not depend on the input. Algorithms with constant space complexity are highly memory-efficient and are often preferred when optimizing for limited memory resources.

Logarithmic space complexity, expressed as $O(\log n)$, indicates that an algorithm's memory usage grows slowly as the input size increases. Logarithmic space algorithms divide the input into smaller segments and process them independently, using only a fraction of the memory required for the full input. These algorithms are efficient in terms of memory usage and are commonly employed in scenarios where memory is a concern.

Linear space complexity, denoted as $O(n)$, means that an algorithm's memory usage grows in direct proportion to the input size. In other words, for every additional input element, the algorithm consumes a fixed amount of memory. While linear space algorithms are straightforward to implement, they may not be suitable for large input sizes, as they can quickly exhaust available memory.

Quadratic space complexity, expressed as O(n^2), signifies that an algorithm's memory usage grows quadratically with the input size. This is often seen in algorithms that involve nested loops or data structures with a high memory overhead. Quadratic space algorithms are generally less memory-efficient and may not scale well with large datasets.

Optimizing space complexity often involves trade-offs with time complexity. Reducing memory usage may require additional computational steps or more complex data structures to achieve the same task. It is crucial to strike a balance between time and space efficiency based on the specific requirements and constraints of the problem at hand.

In situations where memory resources are limited, such as in embedded systems or mobile applications, efficient space utilization is paramount. Developers may need to explore techniques like data compression, in-place algorithms, or memory pooling to minimize memory usage while maintaining acceptable performance.

In contrast, cloud computing environments with ample memory resources may prioritize optimizing for time complexity. In these scenarios, algorithms can use additional memory to store intermediate results or cache frequently accessed data, leading to faster execution times.

Dynamic programming is a technique commonly used to optimize both time and space complexity. By storing and reusing previously computed results, dynamic programming algorithms can reduce redundant calculations and improve efficiency. This technique often leads to linear space complexity, making it suitable for a wide range of applications.

Understanding and analyzing space complexity is an integral part of algorithm design and evaluation. It allows developers to make informed decisions about which algorithms to use in specific situations and how to optimize them for memory-efficient execution. By considering both time and space complexity, you can create algorithms that strike the right balance between resource usage and computational efficiency.

In summary, space complexity and memory usage are essential aspects of algorithm analysis and design. They provide valuable insights into how efficiently an algorithm utilizes memory resources, which is crucial in various computing environments. Optimizing space complexity can lead to more efficient algorithms that perform well under memory constraints, ultimately benefiting both developers and end-users.

Chapter 3: Sorting Algorithms Demystified

Sorting is a fundamental operation in computer science and data processing. It involves arranging a collection of items into a specific order, often based on some criteria or key value. Sorting is ubiquitous in everyday life, from organizing files on a computer to alphabetizing a list of names. In computer science, sorting algorithms play a crucial role in optimizing data retrieval and search operations.

The need for sorting arises in various applications, such as databases, web search engines, and even everyday tasks like maintaining contact lists on smartphones. Sorting allows us to quickly locate information, perform efficient searches, and make data more accessible and readable. Different sorting algorithms have been developed over the years, each with its own advantages, disadvantages, and use cases.

The efficiency of sorting algorithms is a critical consideration, as it determines how quickly and resource-efficiently data can be organized. The time complexity of an algorithm measures how the execution time grows relative to the size of the input data. Sorting algorithms with lower time complexity are preferred for large datasets or real-time applications.

In addition to time complexity, space complexity is another important factor when evaluating sorting algorithms. Space complexity measures the amount of additional memory required by an algorithm as it processes data. Efficient algorithms aim to minimize space complexity to conserve memory resources.

Sorting algorithms can be categorized into various types based on their underlying principles and behaviors. Two primary categories are comparison-based sorting and non-comparison-based sorting. Comparison-based sorting algorithms rely on pairwise comparisons of elements to determine their order. Examples of comparison-based sorting algorithms include bubble sort, insertion sort, selection sort, merge sort, and quicksort.

Non-comparison-based sorting algorithms, on the other hand, do not rely on pairwise comparisons alone. They often exploit specific properties of the data to achieve faster sorting. One notable example is counting sort, which is particularly efficient for sorting integers within a known range.

Stability is another property that distinguishes sorting algorithms. A stable sorting algorithm preserves the relative order of equal elements in the sorted output. Stability can be crucial when sorting records with multiple keys or when maintaining the order of previously sorted data.

Sorting algorithms can also be categorized as internal or external, depending on how they handle data that does not fit entirely in memory. Internal sorting algorithms assume that the entire dataset can be stored in memory, while external sorting algorithms are designed to handle datasets that must be stored on disk or in external storage.

The choice of sorting algorithm depends on several factors, including the size of the dataset, available memory, desired time complexity, and the specific characteristics of the data being sorted. Selecting the right algorithm is essential for achieving optimal performance in various applications.

In this book, we will explore a wide range of sorting algorithms, delving into their principles, implementations, and performance characteristics. We will cover both classic sorting algorithms and more advanced techniques that address specific challenges.

Our journey will begin with some of the simplest sorting algorithms, such as bubble sort, insertion sort, and selection sort. These algorithms provide a foundation for understanding sorting principles and serve as a starting point for exploring more complex methods.

As we progress, we will delve into efficient sorting algorithms like merge sort and quicksort, which are widely used in practice due to their favorable time complexity. These algorithms leverage divide-and-conquer strategies to efficiently sort large datasets.

We will also explore specialized sorting algorithms, including radix sort and bucket sort, which are designed for specific types of data and offer exceptional performance in certain scenarios.

Additionally, we will discuss practical considerations, such as sorting stability, adaptiveness, and the impact of the initial order of data on sorting efficiency. Understanding these factors will help you choose the most suitable sorting algorithm for your applications.

Furthermore, we will examine external sorting techniques, which are essential for handling massive datasets that exceed available memory. External sorting algorithms, like external merge sort, enable efficient sorting of data stored on disk or in external storage.

Throughout our exploration of sorting algorithms, we will provide clear explanations, step-by-step implementations, and real-world examples to illustrate their use and demonstrate their efficiency.

Whether you are a student learning about algorithms, a developer seeking to optimize data processing tasks, or a computer scientist interested in the intricacies of sorting, this book will equip you with the knowledge and skills needed to master sorting algorithms and make informed decisions about their application in diverse contexts.

Sorting is a fundamental operation that underlies many aspects of computing and data analysis. By understanding the principles, characteristics, and trade-offs of various sorting algorithms, you will be well-prepared to tackle sorting challenges and enhance the efficiency of your data processing tasks.

In the realm of sorting algorithms, Quick Sort and Merge Sort are two widely used and highly efficient methods. Quick Sort, also known as partition-exchange sort, is renowned for its speed and is often considered one of the fastest sorting algorithms available. It belongs to the category of comparison-based sorting algorithms, which means it makes pairwise comparisons of elements to determine their order.

Merge Sort, on the other hand, is known for its stability and predictable performance. It is a divide-and-conquer algorithm that breaks the sorting process into smaller, more manageable subproblems. Both Quick Sort and Merge Sort have their unique characteristics, advantages, and use cases.

Let's start by exploring Quick Sort, a sorting algorithm that was developed by Tony Hoare in 1960. Quick Sort is known for its efficiency, and it is often used as the go-to sorting algorithm for many applications. The key idea behind Quick Sort is to partition the input array into two subarrays - one with elements smaller than a chosen pivot element and another with elements greater than the pivot. Once the partitioning is complete, the pivot element is in its final sorted position.

The efficiency of Quick Sort lies in its ability to partition the input array efficiently and recursively sort the subarrays. The partitioning process is achieved through a process called the partition algorithm, which selects a pivot element and rearranges the array so that elements smaller than the pivot come before it, and elements greater than the pivot come after it.

One of the advantages of Quick Sort is that it sorts in-place, meaning it requires minimal additional memory beyond the original array. This makes it memory-efficient and suitable for sorting large datasets with limited memory resources.

The time complexity of Quick Sort depends on the choice of the pivot element and the arrangement of elements in the input array. In the best-case scenario, where the pivot divides the array into roughly equal halves, Quick Sort can achieve a time complexity of $O(n \log n)$. In the worst-case scenario, where the pivot consistently selects the smallest or largest element, the time complexity can degrade to $O(n^2)$. However, with proper pivot selection strategies, Quick Sort can often achieve an average time complexity of $O(n \log n)$, making it a highly efficient choice for many sorting tasks.

Now, let's turn our attention to Merge Sort, another powerful sorting algorithm that is known for its stability and predictable performance. Merge Sort was developed by John von Neumann in 1945, and it is based on the divide-and-conquer paradigm.

The key idea behind Merge Sort is to divide the input array into smaller subarrays until each subarray consists of only one element. These single-element subarrays are then merged together in a series of pairwise comparisons and combinations until the entire array is sorted.

Merge Sort is particularly advantageous when stability and predictability are essential requirements. It ensures the relative order of equal elements remains unchanged, making it suitable for sorting records with multiple keys or maintaining the order of previously sorted data.

One of the notable characteristics of Merge Sort is its consistent time complexity. Regardless of the initial arrangement of elements in the input array, Merge Sort always achieves a time complexity of $O(n \log n)$. This predictability makes it a reliable choice for sorting tasks, especially in scenarios where worst-case performance is a concern.

While Merge Sort is efficient in terms of time complexity, it does require additional memory for the merging process. Each subarray needs temporary storage for merging, which results in a space complexity of $O(n)$. This additional memory usage may be a consideration when working with limited memory resources.

In summary, Quick Sort and Merge Sort are two prominent sorting algorithms that offer different advantages and characteristics. Quick Sort is known for its efficiency and in-place sorting, making it suitable for large datasets and applications with limited memory. Merge Sort, on the other hand, prioritizes stability and predictable time complexity, making it an excellent choice for scenarios where worst-case performance is a concern.

Both algorithms have their strengths and weaknesses, and the choice between them depends on the specific requirements of the sorting task at hand. Understanding the principles and trade-offs of Quick Sort and Merge Sort equips you with valuable tools for optimizing data processing and efficiently sorting data in various computational contexts.

Chapter 4: Searching for Solutions: Search Algorithms

In the world of computer science and data processing, search algorithms are essential tools for finding specific information within a dataset. Search algorithms allow us to locate items, values, or records based on certain criteria or key values. They are fundamental to data retrieval, information retrieval systems, and various applications, from web search engines to database queries.

The need for efficient search algorithms arises in numerous scenarios, such as searching for a specific word in a document, finding a particular record in a database, or locating a file on a computer. The effectiveness and performance of search algorithms significantly impact the speed and accuracy of these operations.

Search algorithms can be categorized into several types based on their underlying principles and behaviors. Two primary categories are linear search and binary search. Linear search, also known as sequential search, examines each item in the dataset one by one until the desired item is found or the entire dataset is searched.

Binary search, on the other hand, is a more efficient approach that is applicable to sorted datasets. It repeatedly divides the dataset in half and eliminates half of the remaining items based on a comparison with the target value. This process continues until the desired item is found or the search concludes that the item is not present.

In addition to linear and binary search, there are various specialized search algorithms designed for specific scenarios and data structures. Some of these algorithms are tailored for searching in unsorted data, while others are optimized for searching in sorted or structured datasets.

Efficiency is a crucial consideration when evaluating search algorithms. The efficiency of a search algorithm is typically measured in terms of its time complexity, which describes how the time required for the search operation scales with the size of the dataset. Search algorithms with lower time complexity are preferred, especially when dealing with large datasets or real-time applications.

Linear search, for instance, has a time complexity of $O(n)$, where n represents the size of the dataset. This means that in the worst case, linear search may need to examine every item in the dataset before finding the desired item. In contrast, binary search has a time complexity of $O(\log n)$, making it much faster for sorted datasets.

Binary search is highly efficient for large datasets, as it eliminates half of the remaining items with each comparison. However, it requires that the dataset is sorted, which may introduce additional preprocessing steps if the data is unsorted.

In addition to time complexity, search algorithms may also have space complexity considerations. Space complexity measures the additional memory or storage required by the algorithm during the search process. Efficient search algorithms aim to minimize space complexity to conserve memory resources.

One of the essential aspects of search algorithms is their adaptability to different data structures and scenarios. For example, search trees and hash tables are data structures that support efficient search operations.

Binary search trees (BSTs) are commonly used for searching in dynamic datasets, where elements can be inserted or deleted. They maintain a sorted order, allowing for efficient binary search operations.

Hash tables, on the other hand, are suitable for scenarios where rapid lookups are required. They use a hash function to map keys to specific positions in an array, enabling constant-time average-case searches.

Beyond the basics of linear and binary search, advanced search algorithms like interpolation search and exponential search provide specialized techniques for specific types of data and search patterns. Interpolation search, for instance, is effective when searching for a value in a dataset with uniform distribution.

In this book, we will explore a wide range of search algorithms, delving into their principles, implementations, and performance characteristics. We will cover classic search algorithms, specialized techniques, and strategies for optimizing search operations.

Our journey will begin with linear search and binary search, providing a solid foundation for understanding search principles. We will explore their efficiency, adaptability, and use cases in various applications.

As we progress, we will delve into advanced search algorithms like interpolation search, exponential search, and other specialized techniques. These algorithms offer unique solutions for specific scenarios and data distributions.

Additionally, we will discuss practical considerations, such as searching in structured data, dealing with duplicates, and optimizing for real-time search performance. Understanding these factors will help you choose the most suitable search algorithm for your applications.

Furthermore, we will examine search in multidimensional data, which is prevalent in fields like geographic information systems (GIS) and image processing. Multidimensional search algorithms provide efficient solutions for locating data points in multi-dimensional space.

Throughout our exploration of search algorithms, we will provide clear explanations, step-by-step implementations, and real-world examples to illustrate their use and demonstrate their efficiency.

Whether you are a student learning about algorithms, a developer seeking to optimize data retrieval tasks, or a computer scientist interested in the intricacies of search, this book will equip you with the knowledge and skills needed to master search algorithms and make informed decisions about their application in diverse computational contexts.

Search algorithms are the foundation of efficient data retrieval and information retrieval. By understanding the principles, characteristics, and trade-offs of various search algorithms, you will be well-prepared to tackle search challenges and enhance the efficiency of your data processing tasks.

In the realm of search algorithms, Binary Search and Hashing are two powerful techniques that excel in different scenarios and offer unique advantages. Binary Search is known for its efficiency in locating a target element within a sorted dataset. It is a divide-and-conquer algorithm that repeatedly divides the dataset in half, eliminating half of the remaining items with each comparison.

One of the key requirements for Binary Search is that the dataset must be sorted in ascending or descending order. This sorted property allows Binary Search to efficiently locate the target element by making intelligent comparisons. The process of Binary Search starts by selecting a midpoint within the dataset and comparing the target element with this midpoint. If the target element is equal to the midpoint, the search is successful, and the index of the element is returned. If the target element is less than the midpoint, the search continues in the left half of the dataset; otherwise, it proceeds in the right half.

This division and comparison process repeats until the target element is found or the search concludes that the element is not present in the dataset. Binary Search's efficiency lies in its ability to eliminate half of the remaining items in each step, resulting in a time complexity of $O(\log n)$, where n represents the size of the dataset.

Binary Search is an ideal choice for searching in large, sorted datasets, where its logarithmic time complexity ensures fast retrieval times. It is commonly used in various applications, such as searching in databases, phone directories, and sorted lists.

However, Binary Search is not suitable for unsorted datasets, as it relies on the sorted property to make informed comparisons. Sorting the dataset beforehand introduces an additional time complexity, which may not be justified in scenarios where the dataset changes frequently.

Hashing, on the other hand, is a technique used to rapidly locate a specific element within a dataset, whether it is sorted or unsorted. Hashing employs a data structure called a hash table, which uses a hash function to map keys to specific positions in an array.

The hash function takes a key as input and calculates a hash code, which determines the index or location in the array where the associated value will be stored. This indexing process enables constant-time average-case searches, making hashing highly efficient for lookups.

Hashing is commonly used in various applications, such as database indexing, caching, and symbol tables. It is particularly useful when rapid access to data is required, and the dataset may not be sorted.

One of the advantages of hashing is its ability to handle unsorted datasets efficiently. Hash tables do not rely on the sorted property of the data, making them suitable for scenarios where the dataset is dynamic and frequently updated.

To illustrate the efficiency of hashing, consider a scenario where you need to store a large collection of phone numbers and associated names. Using a hash table, you can quickly locate a phone number by hashing the associated name and retrieving the corresponding entry from the table.

However, hashing does have certain limitations and considerations. One challenge is handling collisions, which occur when multiple keys produce the same hash code. To address collisions, various collision resolution techniques, such as chaining and open addressing, are employed to ensure that each key maps to a unique location in the hash table.

Another consideration in hashing is the choice of an appropriate hash function. A good hash function should evenly distribute keys across the hash table to minimize collisions and provide efficient access.

In some cases, hash tables may experience performance degradation when the load factor, which measures the ratio of stored elements to the table size, becomes too high. Resizing the hash table or adopting dynamic resizing strategies can help maintain efficient performance.

Binary Search and Hashing are valuable tools in the arsenal of search algorithms, each offering unique benefits. Binary Search excels in scenarios with sorted datasets, providing efficient retrieval with a time complexity of O(log n). Hashing, on the other hand, offers constant-time average-case searches and is ideal for rapid data access, regardless of the dataset's order.

The choice between Binary Search and Hashing depends on the specific requirements of the search task. If you have a sorted dataset and are looking for a specific element, Binary Search may be the preferred choice. If you need fast access to data and the dataset may not be sorted, Hashing is a reliable option.

In this book, we will explore the principles, implementations, and performance characteristics of Binary Search and Hashing in detail. We will delve into real-world examples, case studies, and practical considerations to help you master these essential search techniques.

Our journey will include discussions on hashing collisions, hash function design, load factors, and collision resolution strategies. We will also examine variations of hashing, such as open addressing and double hashing, to expand your understanding of this powerful search technique.

Whether you are a student learning about algorithms, a developer seeking to optimize data retrieval tasks, or a computer scientist interested in the intricacies of search, this book will equip you with the knowledge and skills needed to excel in Binary Search and Hashing and make informed decisions about their application in diverse computational contexts.

Binary Search and Hashing are key components of efficient data retrieval and search operations. By understanding the principles and trade-offs of these search techniques, you will be well-prepared to tackle search challenges and optimize data access in various computational scenarios.

Chapter 5: Dynamic Programming: A Powerful Problem-Solving Tool

In the field of computer science and algorithm design, Dynamic Programming is a powerful technique used to solve a wide range of complex problems. Dynamic Programming, often abbreviated as DP, is not a specific algorithm but rather a general approach to solving problems by breaking them down into smaller subproblems. The key idea behind Dynamic Programming is to store the results of subproblems in memory so that they can be reused when needed, avoiding redundant calculations.

The term "programming" in Dynamic Programming does not refer to computer programming but rather to planning and decision-making. Dynamic Programming is particularly valuable for optimization problems, where the goal is to find the best solution among a set of possible solutions. It is also used in problems that exhibit overlapping subproblems, where the same subproblem is solved multiple times.

The foundation of Dynamic Programming is the concept of recursion, where a problem is solved by solving smaller instances of the same problem. Each time a subproblem is solved, its result is stored in a data structure, such as an array or a memoization table. This stored information allows the algorithm to avoid recomputing the same subproblem in the future, leading to significant time savings.

One of the fundamental techniques in Dynamic Programming is the top-down approach, also known as memoization. In the top-down approach, the problem is solved recursively, and the results of subproblems are stored in memory for future reference. When a subproblem is encountered again, the algorithm first checks if its result is already in memory before recomputing it.

The bottom-up approach, on the other hand, is another common technique in Dynamic Programming. In the bottom-up approach, subproblems are solved in a specific order, starting with the simplest subproblems and building up to the original problem. This approach is often implemented using iterative loops and is typically more space-efficient than the top-down approach.

Dynamic Programming is best understood through examples, and one classic problem that illustrates its principles is the Fibonacci sequence. The Fibonacci sequence is a series of numbers where each number is the sum of the two preceding ones, typically starting with 0 and 1. The sequence begins: 0, 1, 1, 2, 3, 5, 8, 13, 21, and so on.

A straightforward recursive algorithm to calculate the nth Fibonacci number involves repeatedly calling the function for (n-1) and (n-2) until reaching the base cases, which are typically F(0) = 0 and F(1) = 1. However, this recursive approach leads to redundant calculations, as the same Fibonacci numbers are computed multiple times.

Dynamic Programming offers a more efficient solution to the Fibonacci problem. By using memoization or a bottom-up approach, the algorithm can store the results of previously computed Fibonacci numbers and reuse them to calculate the next number in the sequence. This eliminates redundancy and significantly improves the efficiency of the algorithm.

Dynamic Programming is not limited to Fibonacci sequences; it is applicable to a wide variety of problems across different domains. It is commonly used in algorithmic challenges, optimization problems, and tasks involving sequence alignment, graph traversal, and resource allocation.

In the context of optimization problems, Dynamic Programming aims to find the best possible solution while considering various constraints and objectives. One well-known example is the knapsack problem, where a set of items with different values and weights must be selected to maximize the total value while staying within a weight limit.

Dynamic Programming can also be applied to problems in computational biology, such as sequence alignment in DNA or protein sequences. It helps identify the most similar regions between sequences, which is crucial for understanding genetic relationships and functional analysis.

In graph algorithms, Dynamic Programming is used for tasks like finding the shortest path between two nodes in a weighted graph or calculating the maximum flow in a network flow problem. By breaking down these complex problems into smaller subproblems and storing intermediate results, Dynamic Programming enables efficient solutions.

The concept of memoization, which involves storing the results of subproblems in memory, is a fundamental aspect of Dynamic Programming. Memoization can be implemented using various data structures, such as arrays, hash tables, or multidimensional arrays. The choice of data structure depends on the specific problem and the nature of the subproblems.

One important consideration when using Dynamic Programming is defining the recurrence relation, which describes how the solution to a larger problem depends on the solutions to smaller subproblems. The recurrence relation forms the basis for creating the algorithm and is critical for understanding its correctness and efficiency.

Dynamic Programming is a versatile and powerful technique that has widespread applications in computer science and algorithm design. It offers efficient solutions to complex problems by breaking them down into smaller, overlapping subproblems and storing their results in memory. Through examples and practice, you can master the principles of Dynamic Programming and apply them to a wide range of computational challenges.

Dynamic Programming is a versatile technique that can be applied to a wide range of computational problems, from sequence analysis to optimization and resource allocation. Let's explore some concrete examples of Dynamic Programming problems to gain a deeper understanding of its application.

One classic example is the Fibonacci sequence, where each number is the sum of the two preceding ones. To calculate the nth Fibonacci number efficiently, Dynamic Programming can be used to store the results of previously computed Fibonacci numbers and reuse them when needed.

In the context of sequence alignment, Dynamic Programming is applied to problems like the edit distance or Levenshtein distance. Given two strings, the goal is to transform one string into the other with the fewest operations, such as insertions, deletions, or substitutions.

In the domain of computational biology, Dynamic Programming is used for sequence alignment of DNA, RNA, or protein sequences. The Needleman-Wunsch algorithm, for instance, aligns sequences to identify similarities and differences, crucial for understanding genetic relationships and functional analysis.

Another well-known problem addressed by Dynamic Programming is the knapsack problem. In this optimization problem, a set of items with different values and weights must be selected to maximize the total value while staying within a weight limit.

Dynamic Programming also plays a vital role in graph algorithms. For instance, the shortest path problem aims to find the shortest path between two nodes in a weighted graph, and Dynamic Programming algorithms like Dijkstra's or Floyd-Warshall are used to efficiently compute these paths.

Resource allocation problems, such as the job scheduling or task assignment problem, can be tackled using Dynamic Programming. These problems involve assigning limited resources to tasks or jobs to optimize a certain objective, like minimizing completion time or maximizing efficiency.

In computational linguistics, Dynamic Programming is applied to natural language processing tasks like speech recognition and language modeling. Efficient algorithms are used to process and analyze large volumes of text or audio data.

In the field of finance, Dynamic Programming is used for portfolio optimization. Investors seek to allocate their investments among various assets to maximize returns while managing risks, and Dynamic Programming helps find the optimal allocation strategy.

Dynamic Programming also has applications in image processing. One example is image segmentation, where the goal is to partition an image into regions with similar properties, and Dynamic Programming algorithms help identify boundaries between these regions.

In artificial intelligence and machine learning, Dynamic Programming is employed in reinforcement learning algorithms. Agents learn optimal strategies by interacting with an environment and using Dynamic Programming to update their policies based on rewards and penalties.

In game theory, Dynamic Programming is used to solve sequential decision-making problems, such as chess or poker. Algorithms like minimax with alpha-beta pruning optimize strategies by exploring possible moves and outcomes.

Dynamic Programming is also prevalent in robotics for path planning and motion control. Robots use efficient algorithms to navigate through environments, avoiding obstacles and reaching their destinations.

In telecommunications, Dynamic Programming is used for error correction and data compression. Efficient algorithms help transmit and receive data accurately while conserving bandwidth.

In summary, Dynamic Programming is a powerful technique with diverse applications across various fields. It is a versatile tool for solving complex problems efficiently by breaking them down into smaller, overlapping subproblems and storing their results in memory. Whether in biology, finance, linguistics, or robotics, Dynamic Programming plays a crucial role in optimizing processes and making informed decisions in computational tasks.

Chapter 6: Greedy Algorithms: Optimizing for the Best Outcome

In the realm of algorithm design, Greedy Algorithms are a class of algorithms known for their simplicity and efficiency. Greedy Algorithms are used to solve optimization problems where the goal is to find the best solution among a set of choices at each step. The key idea behind Greedy Algorithms is to make the locally optimal choice at each step in the hope that this will lead to a globally optimal solution.

Unlike Dynamic Programming, which considers all possible choices and stores the results of subproblems, Greedy Algorithms focus on making immediate decisions based on the current state of the problem. These algorithms do not backtrack or reconsider choices once made, which can lead to efficient and straightforward solutions.

Greedy Algorithms are particularly suitable for problems that exhibit the greedy-choice property, where making the locally optimal choice at each step ensures that the overall solution is optimal. However, not all optimization problems can be solved optimally using Greedy Algorithms, and careful consideration is required to determine if the greedy approach is appropriate.

One classic example of a problem well-suited for Greedy Algorithms is the coin change problem. Given a set of coin denominations and an amount to be paid, the goal is to find the minimum number of coins needed to make the exact change. Greedy Algorithms, in this case, involve selecting the largest denomination coin that is less than or equal to the remaining amount at each step.

Another example of a Greedy Algorithm is the activity selection problem. In this problem, a set of activities with start and end times are given, and the goal is to select the maximum number of non-overlapping activities. The greedy choice is to always select the activity that finishes first, as this opens up the most opportunities for scheduling other activities.

Greedy Algorithms are also commonly used in scheduling and optimization problems. For instance, in the scheduling of jobs on machines, the goal is to minimize the total completion time of all jobs. A Greedy Algorithm can be employed to assign jobs to machines in a way that minimizes idle time and maximizes efficiency.

In Huffman coding, a data compression technique used in applications like file compression and data transmission, Greedy Algorithms are applied to create optimal variable-length codes for characters. The greedy choice is to merge the two least frequent characters into a single node in a binary tree until all characters are included in the tree.

While Greedy Algorithms offer simplicity and efficiency, they are not always guaranteed to produce an optimal solution. The greedy-choice property, where locally optimal choices lead to global optimality, is a critical condition for the success of Greedy Algorithms. If this property does not hold, a greedy approach may lead to suboptimal or incorrect solutions.

In some cases, Greedy Algorithms can be used to find approximate solutions to optimization problems, even when optimality cannot be guaranteed. These algorithms provide a good balance between simplicity and effectiveness in situations where finding an exact solution is impractical or computationally expensive.

One common example is the traveling salesman problem, where a salesman must visit a set of cities exactly once and return to the starting city while minimizing the total distance traveled. Although finding the optimal solution is NP-hard,

Greedy Algorithms like the nearest neighbor algorithm can quickly produce reasonably good solutions.

In summary, Greedy Algorithms are a class of algorithms used to solve optimization problems by making locally optimal choices at each step. They offer simplicity and efficiency in various applications, including coin change, activity selection, scheduling, Huffman coding, and approximate solutions to complex problems like the traveling salesman problem.

While Greedy Algorithms are powerful and intuitive, it is essential to assess whether the greedy-choice property holds for a specific problem and whether the algorithm is suitable for finding an optimal or approximate solution. Understanding the principles and limitations of Greedy Algorithms is crucial for effectively applying them to various computational challenges.

To understand Greedy Algorithms better, let's explore a few real-world examples where these algorithms can be applied to solve practical problems. One such problem is the "Minimum Spanning Tree" problem in graph theory.

In this problem, we have a weighted, connected graph where each edge has a certain weight. The goal is to find a subset of edges that forms a tree and spans all the vertices while minimizing the total weight of the tree. This tree is called the "Minimum Spanning Tree" (MST).

One well-known algorithm for finding the MST is Kruskal's algorithm, which is a Greedy Algorithm. Kruskal's algorithm starts with an empty set of edges and repeatedly adds the shortest edge that connects two different components (subsets of vertices) in the graph until all vertices are connected.

The Greedy choice in Kruskal's algorithm is to select the shortest available edge that does not create a cycle in the

MST being constructed. This ensures that we are always adding the locally optimal edge with the smallest weight, which leads to a globally optimal MST.

Kruskal's algorithm demonstrates the power of Greedy Algorithms in solving complex problems efficiently. It is used in various applications, such as network design, circuit design, and transportation planning, to find the most cost-effective way to connect components or locations.

Another example of Greedy Algorithms in action is the "Fractional Knapsack Problem." In this problem, we have a set of items, each with a weight and a value, and a knapsack with a maximum weight capacity. The goal is to select a fraction of each item to include in the knapsack in such a way that the total value of the selected items is maximized without exceeding the knapsack's weight limit.

The Greedy choice in the Fractional Knapsack Problem is to select items with the highest value-to-weight ratio first. By prioritizing items that provide the most value for their weight, we maximize the value of the items included in the knapsack.

This Greedy approach works well because it ensures that we are selecting the most valuable items first, optimizing the use of the knapsack's capacity. The Fractional Knapsack Problem has applications in resource allocation, cargo loading, and portfolio optimization.

A classic application of Greedy Algorithms is found in "Dijkstra's Shortest Path Algorithm." Given a weighted graph and a source vertex, Dijkstra's algorithm finds the shortest path from the source vertex to all other vertices in the graph. It uses a priority queue to select and explore vertices in a greedy manner, considering the shortest path discovered so far.

The Greedy choice in Dijkstra's algorithm is to always select the vertex with the shortest known distance from the source and explore its neighbors. By continuously selecting the closest unexplored vertex, the algorithm guarantees that the shortest path to each vertex is discovered correctly.

Dijkstra's algorithm is widely used in network routing, navigation systems, and road network optimization, where finding the shortest path between locations is essential.

Another practical application of Greedy Algorithms is in "Interval Scheduling." In Interval Scheduling, we have a set of tasks, each with a start time and an end time, and the goal is to schedule as many tasks as possible without overlapping.

The Greedy choice in Interval Scheduling is to sort the tasks by their end times and select non-overlapping tasks with the earliest end times. This ensures that we maximize the number of tasks scheduled while avoiding conflicts.

Interval Scheduling is employed in various scheduling scenarios, such as job scheduling, meeting scheduling, and resource allocation, where efficient task scheduling is crucial.

In the domain of data compression, Greedy Algorithms are used in the "Huffman Coding" technique. Huffman Coding is a variable-length prefix coding method used for data compression, where frequently occurring characters are encoded with shorter codes, reducing the overall data size.

The Greedy choice in Huffman Coding is to construct a binary tree, called the Huffman Tree, by repeatedly merging the two least frequent characters into a single node until all characters are included. This results in shorter codes for more frequent characters and longer codes for less frequent characters, ensuring efficient compression.

Huffman Coding is widely used in file compression formats like ZIP and JPEG, where reducing file size without loss of information is essential.

In summary, Greedy Algorithms are powerful tools for solving optimization problems in various fields. They operate by making locally optimal choices at each step, often leading to globally optimal solutions. Examples such as finding Minimum Spanning Trees, solving the Fractional Knapsack Problem, finding shortest paths, interval scheduling, and data compression demonstrate the practical applications of Greedy Algorithms in action.

Understanding the Greedy choice in each problem and its rationale is essential for effectively applying Greedy Algorithms to solve real-world challenges, providing efficient and optimal solutions in many domains.

Chapter 7: Graph Algorithms: Navigating Complex Networks

Graph Theory is a fundamental branch of mathematics and computer science that deals with the study of graphs. A graph is a mathematical abstraction used to represent relationships or connections between objects, which are typically represented as vertices (nodes) and the connections between them as edges.

Graphs are versatile structures that find applications in a wide range of fields, from computer networking and social networks to transportation systems and biology. The study of graphs, known as Graph Theory, provides valuable tools and techniques for analyzing, modeling, and solving problems in various domains.

Graphs can be classified into different types based on their characteristics and properties. One common distinction is between directed and undirected graphs. In an undirected graph, edges have no direction, meaning that the connection between two vertices is symmetric. In contrast, directed graphs, or digraphs, have directed edges, indicating a one-way relationship between vertices.

Another classification is based on whether the graph contains cycles or not. A graph with no cycles is called a tree, and it forms the basis for hierarchical structures in computer science and data organization. Trees have a root node from which all other nodes are reachable through a unique path.

Graphs can also be weighted, where each edge has an associated weight or cost. Weighted graphs are used in various optimization problems, such as finding the shortest path between two vertices or constructing minimum spanning trees.

Graphs are represented visually through diagrams that illustrate vertices as points or circles and edges as lines or arcs connecting the vertices. These visual representations help in understanding the structure and relationships within the graph.

The concept of adjacency is crucial in Graph Theory. Two vertices in a graph are considered adjacent if there is an edge connecting them. The set of all vertices adjacent to a particular vertex is known as its neighborhood.

Graphs can be finite or infinite, depending on the number of vertices and edges. In practical applications, finite graphs are more common and easier to work with.

A special type of graph is a bipartite graph, where the set of vertices can be divided into two disjoint sets such that no two vertices within the same set are adjacent. Bipartite graphs find applications in various areas, including matching problems and network flows.

The degree of a vertex in a graph is the number of edges incident to that vertex. In undirected graphs, the degree is equal to the number of neighbors a vertex has. In directed graphs, vertices have both an in-degree (the number of incoming edges) and an out-degree (the number of outgoing edges).

Graphs can be connected or disconnected. A graph is considered connected if there is a path between any pair of vertices, meaning that all vertices can be reached from any starting vertex. In contrast, disconnected graphs consist of multiple connected components, where no path exists between vertices in different components.

Graphs are not limited to a single application; they are used in various domains. In computer science and networking, graphs model the connections between devices, routers, and nodes in a network. They are essential for routing algorithms, network design, and analyzing network topologies.

In social network analysis, graphs represent relationships between individuals or entities. Nodes in the graph represent individuals, and edges represent connections or interactions. Graph algorithms help identify influential nodes, community structures, and information diffusion patterns in social networks.

In transportation and logistics, graphs are used to model road networks, flight routes, and public transportation systems. Graph algorithms are employed to find the shortest path between locations, optimize transportation routes, and schedule deliveries efficiently.

In biology, graphs represent complex biological systems, such as protein-protein interaction networks, metabolic pathways, and phylogenetic trees. Graph theory helps biologists understand the relationships between biological entities and analyze biological data.

In recommendation systems, graphs are used to model user-item interactions. Nodes represent users and items, and edges represent interactions or preferences. Graph-based recommendation algorithms provide personalized recommendations based on the connections between users and items.

In computer graphics and image processing, graphs are employed to represent pixel neighborhoods, image segmentation, and object recognition. Graph-based algorithms enable the extraction of meaningful structures and features from images.

Graph Theory is not limited to these applications; it finds use in various other fields, including chemistry, linguistics, and operations research. Its versatility and applicability make it a valuable tool for solving complex problems and analyzing relationships in diverse domains.

To summarize, Graph Theory is a branch of mathematics and computer science that deals with the study of graphs, which are mathematical abstractions used to represent relationships between objects. Graphs can be classified based on their properties, such as directed or undirected, weighted or unweighted, and connected or disconnected. Graphs have practical applications in numerous fields, including computer science, social network analysis, transportation, biology, recommendation systems, computer graphics, and more. Understanding the fundamentals of Graph Theory is essential for effectively modeling and solving real-world problems in these domains.

In the field of Graph Theory, several fundamental algorithms are used to analyze and manipulate graphs. These algorithms play a crucial role in solving a wide range of problems across various domains.

One of the most well-known graph algorithms is Depth-First Search (DFS). DFS explores a graph by starting at a source vertex and traversing as deeply as possible along each branch before backtracking. This algorithm is used for tasks such as finding connected components, detecting cycles, and topological sorting.

Depth-First Search can be implemented using recursion or a stack data structure. The key to DFS is marking visited vertices to avoid infinite loops when dealing with cyclic graphs.

Another important algorithm is Breadth-First Search (BFS). BFS explores a graph by visiting all the vertices at the current level before moving on to the next level. It is often used to find the shortest path in an unweighted graph and to perform level-order traversal.

BFS is implemented using a queue data structure. By keeping track of the distance from the source vertex to each visited vertex, BFS can efficiently find the shortest path.

Dijkstra's Shortest Path Algorithm is a widely used algorithm for finding the shortest path in weighted graphs. It works by iteratively selecting the vertex with the smallest tentative distance from the source and relaxing its neighbors. Dijkstra's algorithm ensures that the shortest path to each vertex is found correctly.

One of the key components of Dijkstra's algorithm is a priority queue or a min-heap to efficiently select the next vertex to explore.

Bellman-Ford Algorithm is another algorithm for finding the shortest path in weighted graphs, including graphs with negative edge weights. Unlike Dijkstra's algorithm, Bellman-Ford can handle graphs with negative weight cycles and report their presence.

Bellman-Ford works by iteratively relaxing all edges, ensuring that the shortest distances are gradually refined. This algorithm is valuable for scenarios where negative edge weights may exist, but it is less efficient than Dijkstra's algorithm for graphs without negative cycles.

Prim's Algorithm and Kruskal's Algorithm are used to find the Minimum Spanning Tree (MST) in weighted graphs. A Minimum Spanning Tree is a subgraph that connects all vertices with the minimum possible total edge weight.

Prim's Algorithm starts with an initial vertex and repeatedly adds the edge with the smallest weight that connects a vertex in the MST to a vertex outside the MST.

Kruskal's Algorithm builds the MST by iteratively selecting the smallest available edge that does not create a cycle. Both algorithms ensure that the resulting tree spans all vertices while minimizing the total weight.

Topological Sorting is an algorithm used to find a linear ordering of vertices in a directed acyclic graph (DAG) such that for every directed edge (u, v), vertex u comes before vertex v in the ordering. Topological sorting is essential in scheduling tasks with dependencies, such as project management and job scheduling.

The algorithm works by repeatedly selecting a vertex with no incoming edges (in-degree of zero) and removing it along with its outgoing edges. The process continues until all vertices are included in the ordering.

In network flow problems, the Ford-Fulkerson Algorithm and its variants, such as the Edmonds-Karp Algorithm, are used to find the maximum flow in a flow network. The maximum flow represents the maximum amount of flow that can be sent from a source to a sink while satisfying capacity constraints on the edges.

These algorithms work by repeatedly finding augmenting paths from the source to the sink and increasing the flow along these paths. The process continues until no more augmenting paths can be found.

In addition to these common graph algorithms, there are various other specialized algorithms and techniques for solving specific graph-related problems. Some examples include the Floyd-Warshall Algorithm for all-pairs shortest paths, the Kosaraju Algorithm for strongly connected components, and the Tarjan Algorithm for finding articulation points and bridges.

Graph algorithms are essential tools for solving a wide range of problems in computer science, network design, social network analysis, transportation planning, and many other fields. Understanding the principles and implementations of these algorithms is crucial for effectively analyzing and manipulating graph data structures.

These algorithms leverage various data structures and techniques, such as queues, stacks, priority queues, and dynamic programming, to efficiently explore and process graphs of different types and sizes. By mastering these algorithms, you can tackle complex graph-related challenges and optimize decision-making in diverse computational scenarios.

Chapter 8: Divide and Conquer: Solving Problems Efficiently

In algorithm design and problem-solving, the Divide and Conquer approach is a fundamental strategy used to solve complex problems by breaking them down into smaller, more manageable subproblems. The fundamental idea behind Divide and Conquer is to divide a problem into smaller instances of the same problem, conquer these smaller instances through recursive solving, and then combine their solutions to form the solution to the original problem.

This approach is often associated with algorithm design paradigms and has been instrumental in solving a wide range of problems in computer science and mathematics. Divide and Conquer is not a specific algorithm but rather a problem-solving technique that can be applied to a diverse set of problems.

The Divide and Conquer process typically consists of three main steps: dividing the problem, conquering the subproblems, and combining their solutions. Each of these steps plays a critical role in the overall approach.

The first step, dividing the problem, involves breaking the original problem into smaller subproblems that are of the same type as the original problem. These subproblems should be simpler and more manageable than the original problem and ideally share a similar structure or nature.

The second step, conquering the subproblems, entails solving the smaller subproblems individually. This is often done recursively, as the subproblems may themselves be divided into even smaller sub-subproblems, and so on, until the sub-subproblems become simple enough to be solved directly.

The third step, combining the solutions, involves taking the solutions to the subproblems and combining them in a way that produces the solution to the original problem. The specific method of combination depends on the nature of the problem being solved.

One classic example of a problem that can be solved using the Divide and Conquer approach is the "Merge Sort" algorithm. Merge Sort is a sorting algorithm that efficiently sorts a list of elements by dividing it into two smaller sublists, sorting these sublists, and then merging the sorted sublists back together to produce a sorted result.

In Merge Sort, the "dividing" step involves splitting the input list into two equal-sized sublists (or approximately equal-sized, in the case of an odd number of elements). The "conquering" step recursively sorts each of these sublists by applying the Merge Sort algorithm to them. Finally, the "combining" step merges the sorted sublists back together into a single sorted list.

Merge Sort's Divide and Conquer strategy results in a highly efficient sorting algorithm with a time complexity of O(n log n), where n is the number of elements in the input list. This makes Merge Sort suitable for sorting large datasets.

Another well-known example of a problem that employs Divide and Conquer is the "Quick Sort" algorithm. Quick Sort is a highly efficient, in-place sorting algorithm that also relies on dividing the input into smaller sublists, sorting them, and then combining them.

In Quick Sort, the dividing step involves selecting a pivot element from the input list and partitioning the list into two sublists: one containing elements less than the pivot and another containing elements greater than the pivot. The conquering step recursively sorts both sublists, and the combining step is relatively simple, as the sorted sublists can be concatenated together to form the final sorted list.

Quick Sort's Divide and Conquer approach yields an average-case time complexity of O(n log n), making it one of the fastest sorting algorithms available.

Divide and Conquer principles are not limited to sorting algorithms; they are widely applicable to a diverse array of problems. For instance, the "Binary Search" algorithm uses the Divide and Conquer approach to efficiently find a target element in a sorted array.

In Binary Search, the dividing step involves selecting a middle element in the array and comparing it to the target element. Depending on the comparison result, the algorithm narrows down the search to either the left or right subarray. The conquering step recursively applies the Binary Search algorithm to the selected subarray, effectively dividing the search space in half with each iteration.

The "Closest Pair of Points" problem is another example that leverages Divide and Conquer. In this problem, the goal is to find the two closest points among a set of points in a 2D plane.

The Divide and Conquer approach involves dividing the set of points into two halves along the x-axis and recursively finding the closest pairs in each half. The combining step considers pairs that may cross the dividing line and combines them with the minimum distance pairs from each half.

Divide and Conquer principles also play a significant role in algorithmic paradigms such as "Dynamic Programming" and "Strassen's Matrix Multiplication." Dynamic Programming breaks down complex problems into overlapping subproblems and stores their solutions to avoid redundant computations, while Strassen's Matrix Multiplication divides large matrices into smaller submatrices and combines them using a more efficient method than the traditional matrix multiplication algorithm.

In summary, Divide and Conquer is a powerful problem-solving technique used to break down complex problems into smaller, more manageable subproblems. It involves three main steps: dividing the problem, conquering the subproblems, and combining their solutions. This approach has been applied to a wide range of problems, including sorting algorithms like Merge Sort and Quick Sort, searching algorithms like Binary Search, and optimization problems like finding the closest pair of points. Understanding the principles of Divide and Conquer is essential for effectively solving complex computational problems in various domains.

In the realm of computer science and mathematics, recursive problem solving is a powerful and fundamental approach used to tackle complex problems by breaking them down into simpler instances of the same problem. Recursion is a technique where a function or algorithm calls itself to solve a problem that can be divided into smaller, more manageable subproblems.

The essence of recursive problem solving lies in its ability to transform a complex problem into a series of simpler, similar subproblems, often leading to elegant and efficient solutions. Recursion is a fundamental concept in algorithm design and is commonly used in various programming languages.

One of the most classic examples of recursive problem solving is the computation of factorial numbers. The factorial of a non-negative integer n, denoted as n!, is the product of all positive integers from 1 to n. The recursive definition of factorial is n! = n * (n-1)!, with the base case being 0! = 1.

In this recursive approach, calculating the factorial of a number is reduced to calculating the factorial of a smaller number (n-1) and then multiplying it by n. This recursive process continues until the base case (0!) is reached, at which point the recursion terminates.

Recursive problem solving relies on two essential components: the base case and the recursive case. The base case defines when the recursion should stop and serves as the termination condition. In the case of factorial, the base case is when n equals 0, and the factorial is defined as 1.

The recursive case defines how the problem is divided into smaller subproblems and how the results of these subproblems are combined to solve the original problem. For factorial, the recursive case defines that n! is computed by multiplying n with (n-1)!, where (n-1)! is a smaller subproblem.

Another classic example of recursion is the computation of the Fibonacci sequence. The Fibonacci sequence is a series of numbers where each number is the sum of the two preceding ones, typically starting with 0 and 1. The recursive definition of Fibonacci is $F(n) = F(n-1) + F(n-2)$, with base cases $F(0) = 0$ and $F(1) = 1$.

Using this recursive definition, the calculation of Fibonacci numbers can be expressed as a recursive algorithm. To compute $F(n)$, the algorithm recursively computes $F(n-1)$ and $F(n-2)$ until the base cases are reached.

Recursion is not limited to mathematical problems but is also a powerful tool for solving various computational challenges. For instance, recursive algorithms are frequently used in tree and graph traversal. In the context of binary trees, a recursive algorithm can perform in-order, pre-order, or post-order traversals by recursively visiting the left and right subtrees of a node.

Recursive algorithms are also used in solving problems like finding the shortest path in a graph using Depth-First Search (DFS) or Breadth-First Search (BFS). These graph traversal algorithms explore the graph by recursively visiting neighboring nodes, marking them as visited, and continuing the traversal until the destination is reached or all reachable nodes are explored.

Dynamic programming is another area where recursion is a fundamental technique. Dynamic programming involves solving complex problems by breaking them down into overlapping subproblems and storing the results of these subproblems in a table or memoization array. The Fibonacci example can be optimized using dynamic programming by storing previously computed Fibonacci numbers and avoiding redundant calculations.

Recursive problem solving is also prevalent in sorting algorithms like Merge Sort and Quick Sort. Merge Sort divides an array into two halves, recursively sorts them, and then combines them, while Quick Sort selects a pivot element, divides the array into two subarrays, recursively sorts them, and combines them using the pivot.

In addition to its power and versatility, recursive problem solving also comes with some considerations and potential challenges. One of these challenges is ensuring that the recursion terminates, which requires defining clear base cases that provide a stopping condition. Failure to define base cases properly can lead to infinite recursion and stack overflow errors.

Another consideration is the efficiency of recursive algorithms, as they can have higher time and space complexity compared to iterative approaches. Recursion involves function calls and a call stack, which can consume additional memory and result in slower execution compared to iterative solutions for certain problems.

Despite these challenges, recursion remains a valuable and elegant approach to problem solving. It is widely used in programming, mathematics, and computer science to address problems that exhibit self-similar or recursive structures.

In summary, recursive problem solving is a fundamental approach in computer science and mathematics that involves breaking down complex problems into simpler instances of the same problem. Recursion is characterized by its use of a base case to determine when to stop the recursion and a recursive case that defines how to divide the problem into smaller subproblems and combine their solutions. Recursive problem solving is used in various domains, including mathematics, tree and graph traversal, dynamic programming, and sorting algorithms, and provides elegant solutions to a wide range of challenges.

Chapter 9: Exploring Data Structures for Algorithmic Efficiency

In the world of computer science and data management, data structures are fundamental concepts that play a crucial role in organizing, storing, and manipulating data efficiently. A data structure is a specialized format or arrangement for storing and organizing data in a computer's memory or storage devices.

Data structures serve as the building blocks for designing and implementing algorithms and solving a wide range of computational problems. They are essential tools for computer scientists and software engineers, allowing them to manage and access data in various ways, depending on the specific requirements of a problem or application.

One of the simplest and most commonly used data structures is the array. An array is a collection of elements, each identified by an index or a key, that can hold values of the same data type. Arrays provide direct and efficient access to their elements, making them suitable for tasks like storing a list of numbers, characters, or objects.

While arrays are straightforward, their size is typically fixed when created, which can limit their flexibility. To overcome this limitation, dynamic arrays, such as ArrayLists in Java or Vectors in C++, are used. Dynamic arrays can grow or shrink in size during runtime, making them more versatile for managing data.

Linked lists are another fundamental data structure. A linked list consists of a sequence of nodes, each containing data and a reference or pointer to the next node in the list. This structure allows for efficient insertion and removal of elements at any position within the list.

There are different types of linked lists, including singly linked lists (where each node points to the next node), doubly linked lists (where each node points to both the next and previous nodes), and circular linked lists (where the last node points back to the first node).

Stacks and queues are specialized data structures that impose specific rules on how elements are added or removed. A stack follows the Last-In-First-Out (LIFO) principle, where the last element added is the first to be removed. Stacks are commonly used for tasks like function call management in programming languages.

On the other hand, a queue adheres to the First-In-First-Out (FIFO) principle, meaning that the first element added is the first to be removed. Queues are often employed in scenarios such as task scheduling and job management.

Trees are hierarchical data structures that consist of nodes connected by edges. Each tree has a root node from which all other nodes descend. Nodes in a tree can have child nodes, and nodes with no children are called leaf nodes.

Binary trees are a specific type of tree structure where each node has, at most, two children. Binary search trees (BSTs) are binary trees with the property that all nodes in the left subtree have values less than the root node, and all nodes in the right subtree have values greater than the root node. Balanced binary search trees, like AVL trees and Red-Black trees, maintain balance to ensure efficient operations like insertion, deletion, and searching.

Heaps are specialized binary trees used in priority queue implementations. In a max-heap, each parent node has a value greater than or equal to the values of its children, making the maximum value accessible at the root. In a min-heap, each parent node has a value less than or equal to the values of its children, making the minimum value accessible at the root.

Graphs are versatile data structures that represent relationships or connections between objects. A graph consists of nodes (vertices) and edges that connect pairs of nodes. Graphs can be directed (edges have a direction) or undirected (edges have no direction), weighted (edges have associated values), or unweighted (edges have no values).

Graphs are used to model complex systems, including social networks, transportation networks, and computer networks. Algorithms like Depth-First Search (DFS) and Breadth-First Search (BFS) are essential for traversing and analyzing graphs.

Hash tables provide fast and efficient data retrieval by mapping keys to values through a hash function. A hash function takes an input (the key) and computes a fixed-size value (the hash code) that represents the key. Hash tables store key-value pairs and use the hash code to index and retrieve values.

Hash tables offer constant-time average-case complexity for insertion, deletion, and retrieval operations when the hash function distributes keys evenly. Collisions occur when two keys produce the same hash code, which is resolved using techniques like chaining or open addressing.

Trie (pronounced "try") is a tree-like data structure used to store and search for a dynamic set of strings or keys. In a trie, each node represents a character or a part of a string, and the path from the root node to a leaf node represents a complete string.

Tries are efficient for tasks like autocomplete suggestions, spell checking, and searching for words in dictionaries.

Understanding the fundamentals of these data structures is essential for effective problem solving and algorithm design in computer science. Each data structure has unique characteristics, advantages, and use cases, making them valuable tools for managing and processing data efficiently.

Additionally, the choice of an appropriate data structure can significantly impact the performance and scalability of software applications. By mastering the principles and applications of data structures, computer scientists and software engineers can design efficient algorithms and build robust and high-performance software systems. Advanced data structures represent a higher level of complexity and sophistication in organizing and managing data in computer science and software engineering. While fundamental data structures like arrays, linked lists, and trees provide essential building blocks, advanced data structures offer specialized solutions for addressing complex computational challenges.

One such advanced data structure is the hash map, also known as a hash table. Hash maps provide fast data retrieval by associating keys with values through a hash function. This hash function computes a unique index or address for each key, allowing efficient storage and retrieval of values based on their associated keys.

Hash maps are commonly used to implement data structures like dictionaries, sets, and caches. They offer average-case constant-time complexity for insertion, deletion, and retrieval operations when the hash function distributes keys evenly.

However, handling collisions, where two keys produce the same hash code, requires collision resolution techniques like chaining or open addressing. Advanced hash map implementations, such as hash maps with open addressing or cuckoo hashing, further optimize collision resolution for high-performance applications.

Another advanced data structure is the B-tree. B-trees are balanced tree structures designed for efficient disk-based storage and retrieval of large datasets. They have a fixed maximum degree, ensuring balanced trees with a predictable height.

B-trees are commonly used in database systems and file systems to manage and search large datasets efficiently. Their balanced structure allows for efficient insertion, deletion, and searching operations, making them suitable for scenarios where data is stored on disk and needs to be accessed sequentially.

Red-Black trees are another balanced tree structure used to maintain dynamic sets of data. They are a type of self-balancing binary search tree with properties that ensure the tree remains balanced after insertions and deletions. Red-Black trees offer guaranteed logarithmic height, leading to efficient search and update operations.

Splay trees are a specialized binary search tree that self-adjusts during operations to optimize frequently accessed nodes. When a node is accessed or modified, a splay operation is performed, moving the accessed node to the root of the tree. This restructuring allows frequently accessed nodes to be quickly accessed in future operations, resulting in amortized constant time for frequently accessed elements.

Advanced data structures extend beyond trees and hash tables. Fenwick trees, also known as binary indexed trees (BITs), are used to efficiently update and query prefix sums in arrays. They are especially useful in scenarios like range queries and cumulative frequency counting.

Trie structures, which were briefly mentioned earlier, are advanced data structures used for storing and searching dynamic sets of strings or keys. Tries are tree-like structures where each node represents a character or part of a string. They offer efficient autocomplete suggestions, spell checking, and dictionary searches.

Skip lists are a probabilistic data structure designed to provide efficient searching, insertion, and deletion operations. They consist of multiple linked lists with varying levels of granularity. Skip lists offer an alternative to balanced trees and can achieve similar average-case performance without the complexities of tree balancing.

Self-balancing binary search trees, such as AVL trees and splay trees, are advanced data structures that automatically adjust their structure during insertions and deletions to ensure a balanced tree. These structures maintain logarithmic height, leading to efficient search and update operations.

In the context of graph theory, advanced data structures like adjacency lists and adjacency matrices are used to represent graphs and efficiently perform graph-related operations. Adjacency lists store each vertex's neighbors in a linked list or an array, making them suitable for sparse graphs. Adjacency matrices use a two-dimensional array to represent edges between vertices, making them suitable for dense graphs.

In addition to the fundamental and advanced data structures mentioned, there are numerous specialized data structures tailored to specific applications and domains. For instance, spatial data structures like quad trees and k-d trees are used for efficient spatial indexing and range queries in geographic information systems (GIS) and computer graphics.

Bloom filters are probabilistic data structures used to test whether an element is a member of a set, with potential false positives. They are commonly employed in scenarios like data deduplication, spell checking, and web caching.

Suffix trees and suffix arrays are advanced data structures used in string matching and text processing. They enable efficient substring searches, pattern matching, and text indexing, making them valuable in fields like bioinformatics, natural language processing, and information retrieval.

Understanding advanced data structures and their applications is crucial for solving complex computational problems efficiently. These data structures offer specialized solutions for diverse challenges, from optimizing data retrieval to managing large datasets and handling complex data relationships.

Selecting the appropriate data structure for a specific problem or application can greatly impact the performance, scalability, and maintainability of software systems. Advanced data structures are essential tools for computer scientists and software engineers seeking to design high-performance algorithms and build robust and efficient software solutions.

Chapter 10: Beyond the Basics: Advanced Algorithmic Concepts

Advanced algorithmic paradigms represent sophisticated approaches to problem-solving in computer science and related fields. These paradigms go beyond basic techniques and provide powerful tools for tackling complex computational challenges.

One such advanced paradigm is "Dynamic Programming." Dynamic Programming is a technique that breaks down complex problems into simpler overlapping subproblems and solves each subproblem only once, storing its solution for future reference. By avoiding redundant computations, Dynamic Programming can significantly improve the efficiency of algorithms.

Dynamic Programming is widely used in problems where optimal solutions involve making choices at each step, such as finding the shortest path in a graph, optimizing resource allocation, or solving recurrence relations. Notable examples of Dynamic Programming algorithms include Dijkstra's Algorithm for shortest paths and the Knapsack Problem for resource allocation.

Another advanced paradigm is "Greedy Algorithms." Greedy Algorithms make locally optimal choices at each step to construct a globally optimal solution. These algorithms are intuitive, easy to implement, and often provide near-optimal solutions to problems.

Greedy Algorithms are applied to various scenarios, such as finding the minimum spanning tree of a graph using Prim's or Kruskal's Algorithm, or solving the Huffman coding problem for data compression. While Greedy Algorithms offer simplicity and efficiency, they may not always guarantee the best possible solution and require careful analysis to ensure correctness.

"Divide and Conquer" is a fundamental algorithmic paradigm that divides a problem into smaller, more manageable subproblems, solves each subproblem independently, and then combines their solutions to solve the original problem. Divide and Conquer is a versatile approach used in various fields, including sorting algorithms like Merge Sort and Quick Sort, as well as fast Fourier transform algorithms for signal processing.

Advanced algorithmic paradigms also include "Randomized Algorithms," which introduce randomness or probability into the algorithm's decision-making process. Randomized Algorithms are valuable when dealing with uncertainty or when deterministic solutions are impractical or infeasible.

Examples of Randomized Algorithms include the Monte Carlo method for approximating numerical values, randomized primality testing, and algorithms for generating random permutations or graphs.

"Parallel Algorithms" represent a paradigm focused on designing algorithms that can execute multiple operations simultaneously. Parallel Algorithms are essential in the context of modern computing systems with multi-core processors, distributed computing, and high-performance computing clusters.

Parallel Algorithms aim to achieve better performance by utilizing parallelism to solve problems faster or process large datasets more efficiently. Examples include parallel sorting algorithms, parallel matrix multiplication, and parallel graph algorithms.

"Online Algorithms" are a class of algorithms that make decisions sequentially, often with limited information about future inputs. Online Algorithms are commonly used in situations where data arrives incrementally, and decisions must be made without complete knowledge of future data.

Online Algorithms are applied in online scheduling, competitive analysis, and caching algorithms. They require algorithms to make adaptive and efficient decisions as new data becomes available.

In the realm of advanced algorithmic paradigms, "Approximation Algorithms" play a crucial role. Approximation Algorithms are used when finding an exact solution to a problem is computationally intractable or requires excessive time or resources.

These algorithms aim to find near-optimal solutions within a reasonable amount of time, often sacrificing precision for efficiency. Approximation Algorithms are commonly used in optimization problems like the Traveling Salesman Problem, where finding an exact solution for large datasets is impractical.

Advanced algorithmic paradigms also include "Online Learning Algorithms" used in machine learning and artificial intelligence. Online Learning Algorithms adapt to new data in real-time and update their models continuously.

These algorithms are used in scenarios like online advertising, recommendation systems, and predictive analytics. They enable systems to learn and improve from incoming data, making them valuable in dynamic and evolving environments.

"Parallel Algorithms" focus on designing algorithms that can execute multiple operations simultaneously. Parallel Algorithms are essential in modern computing systems with multi-core processors, distributed computing, and high-performance computing clusters.

Parallel Algorithms aim to achieve better performance by utilizing parallelism to solve problems faster or process large datasets more efficiently. Examples include parallel sorting algorithms, parallel matrix multiplication, and parallel graph algorithms.

"Online Algorithms" are a class of algorithms that make decisions sequentially, often with limited information about future inputs. Online Algorithms are commonly used in situations where data arrives incrementally, and decisions must be made without complete knowledge of future data.

Online Algorithms are applied in online scheduling, competitive analysis, and caching algorithms. They require algorithms to make adaptive and efficient decisions as new data becomes available.

In the realm of advanced algorithmic paradigms, "Approximation Algorithms" play a crucial role. Approximation Algorithms are used when finding an exact solution to a problem is computationally intractable or requires excessive time or resources.

These algorithms aim to find near-optimal solutions within a reasonable amount of time, often sacrificing precision for efficiency. Approximation Algorithms are commonly used in optimization problems like the Traveling Salesman Problem, where finding an exact solution for large datasets is impractical.

Advanced algorithmic paradigms also include "Online Learning Algorithms" used in machine learning and artificial intelligence. Online Learning Algorithms adapt to new data in real-time and update their models continuously.

These algorithms are used in scenarios like online advertising, recommendation systems, and predictive analytics. They enable systems to learn and improve from incoming data, making them valuable in dynamic and evolving environments.

In summary, advanced algorithmic paradigms encompass a diverse set of techniques and approaches that extend beyond basic problem-solving methods. These paradigms provide powerful tools for addressing complex computational challenges in various fields, from computer science and optimization to machine learning and artificial intelligence.

Each paradigm offers unique insights and solutions to problems, allowing algorithm designers and researchers to tackle real-world problems efficiently and effectively.

Understanding and mastering these advanced algorithmic paradigms is essential for computer scientists, engineers, and researchers seeking to push the boundaries of computational capability and develop innovative solutions to today's complex and ever-evolving challenges.

Handling complex algorithmic challenges is an integral part of computer science and software engineering, requiring a deep understanding of advanced algorithms and problem-solving techniques. These challenges often arise when dealing with large datasets, intricate data structures, optimization problems, and real-world applications.

One of the key aspects of addressing complex algorithmic challenges is algorithm design. Algorithm design involves creating efficient and effective algorithms that can efficiently solve specific problems. This process requires a comprehensive understanding of the problem, its constraints, and potential trade-offs.

Complex algorithmic challenges often involve optimization problems where the goal is to find the best solution among many possible options. Optimization algorithms aim to minimize or maximize a certain objective function while adhering to given constraints.

For example, in the field of logistics, the traveling salesman problem (TSP) is a classic optimization problem where the objective is to find the shortest possible route that visits a set of cities and returns to the starting city. Solving such problems requires advanced optimization techniques like integer linear programming, genetic algorithms, or simulated annealing.

In handling complex algorithmic challenges, it's crucial to consider algorithmic efficiency. Efficient algorithms can significantly reduce execution time and resource consumption, making them suitable for large-scale and real-time applications.

Efficiency is often measured in terms of time complexity, which quantifies the number of basic operations an algorithm performs relative to the input size. Common notations used to describe time complexity include O-notation, Θ-notation, and Ω-notation.

For example, an algorithm with a time complexity of O(n log n) is more efficient than one with O(n^2) when dealing with large datasets because it scales better.

Complex algorithmic challenges may also involve handling dynamic or streaming data. In such scenarios, algorithms must adapt to changing data and provide timely responses.

Streaming algorithms, such as the Count-Min Sketch or reservoir sampling, are designed to process data on the fly and maintain approximate statistics without storing the entire dataset.

Furthermore, distributed algorithms play a crucial role in addressing complex challenges related to scalability and parallel processing. Distributed algorithms distribute computation and data across multiple nodes or processors to tackle large-scale problems efficiently.

Graph algorithms are fundamental in handling complex algorithmic challenges, especially in fields like social network analysis, recommendation systems, and network optimization. Algorithms like breadth-first search (BFS) and depth-first search (DFS) are used to traverse and analyze graphs, while graph partitioning algorithms aim to divide large graphs into smaller, manageable components.

Machine learning and data mining techniques are increasingly applied to complex algorithmic challenges, especially when dealing with large and high-dimensional datasets. Algorithms like k-means clustering, support vector machines, and deep neural networks are used for tasks such as classification, regression, and clustering.

When facing optimization problems, metaheuristic algorithms like genetic algorithms, simulated annealing, and particle swarm optimization offer alternative approaches to finding near-optimal solutions in complex search spaces.

Complex algorithmic challenges may also involve dealing with uncertainty and probabilistic models. Monte Carlo methods, Markov Chain Monte Carlo (MCMC), and Bayesian networks are used to estimate probabilities, simulate stochastic processes, and make decisions in uncertain environments.

Furthermore, algorithmic challenges related to cybersecurity and cryptography require advanced techniques for securing data, authenticating users, and protecting information from unauthorized access.

In handling cryptographic challenges, algorithms like RSA, AES, and elliptic curve cryptography are used to ensure the confidentiality and integrity of data in various applications, including secure communication and digital signatures.

Real-world applications of complex algorithms extend beyond traditional computer science domains. In computational biology, algorithms for sequence alignment, phylogenetic tree construction, and protein structure prediction are vital for understanding genetic information and advancing medical research.

In finance, algorithms for portfolio optimization, risk assessment, and algorithmic trading play a crucial role in managing investments and financial transactions.

Furthermore, complex algorithmic challenges in natural language processing involve tasks like machine translation, sentiment analysis, and speech recognition, where algorithms must understand and generate human language effectively.

Addressing complex algorithmic challenges also requires attention to algorithmic correctness and robustness. Algorithm correctness ensures that an algorithm produces the correct output for all possible inputs and scenarios.

Formal methods, such as proof-based approaches and model checking, are used to rigorously verify the correctness of algorithms and software systems.

Robustness involves designing algorithms that can handle unexpected or erroneous inputs gracefully, minimizing the risk of failures or vulnerabilities.

Complex algorithmic challenges often require interdisciplinary collaboration between computer scientists, domain experts, and researchers from various fields. Solving complex problems may involve adapting existing algorithms, developing new ones, or combining multiple techniques to achieve the desired outcome.

Moreover, algorithmic challenges frequently require trade-offs between different factors, such as time complexity, space complexity, and accuracy. Algorithm designers must carefully weigh these trade-offs based on the specific requirements and constraints of the problem.

In summary, handling complex algorithmic challenges is a multidimensional task that involves algorithm design, optimization, efficiency, adaptability, and correctness. These challenges span various domains, from optimization and machine learning to distributed computing and cryptography.

Addressing complex algorithmic challenges often involves combining diverse techniques and interdisciplinary collaboration to find innovative solutions that can tackle real-world problems efficiently and effectively.

BOOK 2
MASTERING ALGORITHMS
FROM BASICS TO EXPERT LEVEL

ROB BOTWRIGHT

Chapter 1: Algorithmic Fundamentals for Beginners

In the realm of computer science and information technology, algorithms are the fundamental building blocks that power the digital world we live in today. They are step-by-step instructions that guide computers to perform specific tasks, solve problems, and make decisions.

Algorithms form the core of software applications, search engines, data analysis, and countless other computational processes that shape our daily lives. Understanding algorithms is essential for anyone working in the field of computer science, from beginners to experts.

This introduction aims to provide a glimpse into the world of algorithms, their significance, and their role in solving a wide range of problems.

Algorithms are, in essence, recipes for solving problems in a systematic and efficient manner. They are like the instructions in a cookbook that guide a chef to prepare a delicious meal.

Algorithms are not exclusive to the digital world; they exist in various forms in our everyday lives. For example, when you follow a set of directions to reach a destination, you are essentially executing an algorithm.

Algorithms can be simple or highly complex, depending on the problem they are designed to solve. From sorting a list of numbers to predicting weather patterns or even playing chess at a grandmaster level, algorithms are at the heart of these processes.

One of the key characteristics of algorithms is that they are deterministic. This means that when you provide the same input to an algorithm, it will produce the same output every time.

For example, if you give a sorting algorithm a list of numbers, it will arrange them in a specific order based on its rules. No matter how many times you repeat the process with the same input, the result will always be the same.

Algorithms are also precise and unambiguous. They leave no room for interpretation or guesswork. Every step in an algorithm is well-defined and clearly specified.

The precision of algorithms is crucial because it ensures that computers can execute them without any misunderstandings or errors. Even a tiny mistake or ambiguity in an algorithm's instructions can lead to incorrect results.

Efficiency is another critical aspect of algorithms. Efficient algorithms are designed to perform their tasks using the least amount of resources, such as time and memory. Efficiency is essential in today's fast-paced digital world, where we often need results quickly.

To illustrate the importance of efficiency, consider a search engine that needs to process billions of web pages in seconds to provide you with relevant search results. Without efficient algorithms, this would be an impossible task.

Algorithms come in various forms, each tailored to a specific type of problem. For example, sorting algorithms arrange a list of items in a particular order, while search algorithms help you find an item within a collection.

Other types of algorithms include graph algorithms for analyzing relationships between data points, dynamic programming for solving optimization problems, and machine learning algorithms for making predictions based on data.

The field of algorithms is vast and continually evolving, with new algorithms being developed to address emerging challenges. As technology advances, algorithms become more sophisticated and powerful, enabling us to tackle complex problems that were once considered insurmountable.

When studying algorithms, it's essential to analyze their performance characteristics. This analysis helps us understand how an algorithm behaves under different circumstances and how it scales when dealing with larger datasets.

One common way to measure an algorithm's performance is through time complexity analysis. Time complexity provides an estimate of the amount of time an algorithm will take to complete its task as a function of the input size.

Another aspect of performance analysis is space complexity, which measures the amount of memory or storage an algorithm requires as a function of the input size.

By understanding these complexities, we can make informed decisions when choosing the right algorithm for a particular problem.

The study of algorithms is not limited to theoretical analysis. It also involves practical implementation and testing. Programmers and computer scientists write code to implement algorithms and verify their correctness and efficiency through experimentation.

Algorithms play a crucial role in a wide range of applications and industries. For example, in the field of data science, algorithms are used to analyze large datasets, make predictions, and extract valuable insights.

In finance, algorithms are employed for high-frequency trading, risk assessment, and portfolio optimization. They enable financial institutions to make informed decisions in real-time.

Algorithms are also vital in the realm of artificial intelligence and machine learning. They power recommendation systems, natural language processing, and image recognition, making our digital experiences more personalized and intelligent.

In the healthcare industry, algorithms are used for medical imaging analysis, drug discovery, and patient data management. They contribute to faster and more accurate diagnoses and treatment plans.

Algorithms are behind the scenes in online advertising, determining which ads to show based on user behavior and preferences. They optimize ad placement to maximize revenue for advertisers and publishers.

Algorithms also play a role in transportation and logistics, optimizing routes for delivery trucks, managing traffic signals, and reducing fuel consumption.

In the field of robotics, algorithms control the movements and actions of autonomous robots, enabling them to navigate environments, perform tasks, and interact with humans.

The impact of algorithms extends to cybersecurity, where they protect computer systems from threats and vulnerabilities. Security algorithms encrypt data, verify user identities, and detect suspicious activities.

As we navigate the digital age, algorithms are continually shaping our interactions with technology and the world around us. They are at the heart of the digital revolution, driving innovations and transformations across various industries.

To conclude, algorithms are the foundation of computer science and technology. They are essential tools for solving problems, optimizing processes, and making informed decisions in a wide range of applications.

Whether you're a beginner exploring the basics of algorithms or an expert delving into advanced algorithmic techniques, the journey into the world of algorithms is a fascinating and rewarding one.

As we delve deeper into this subject throughout this book, we will explore various types of algorithms, their applications, and the principles that guide their design and analysis.

Understanding algorithms empowers us to harness the power of computation, tackle complex challenges, and shape the future of technology and innovation.

Basic algorithmic concepts are the fundamental principles that underlie the design and analysis of algorithms, forming the bedrock of computer science and software engineering. These concepts provide the foundation upon which more advanced algorithmic techniques and strategies are built.

At its core, an algorithm is a sequence of well-defined steps or instructions that solve a particular problem or perform a specific task. These instructions are typically expressed in a programming language and can be executed by a computer or other computational device.

One of the primary goals of algorithms is to provide a systematic and efficient approach to problem-solving. By following a set of precise instructions, algorithms enable us to solve problems methodically and consistently.

Algorithms are used in a wide range of applications, from sorting and searching data to optimizing processes, making decisions, and performing complex computations. Understanding basic algorithmic concepts is essential for anyone involved in computer science, programming, data analysis, or any field that relies on computational problem-solving.

One of the fundamental concepts in algorithm design is the notion of correctness. An algorithm is considered correct if it produces the desired output for all valid inputs and adheres to its specifications.

Ensuring the correctness of an algorithm is a critical aspect of the design process. Errors or bugs in algorithms can lead to incorrect results and unexpected behavior, which can have significant consequences in real-world applications.

Algorithm design also involves considering efficiency. Efficient algorithms are designed to use the least amount of computational resources, such as time and memory, to solve a problem.

Efficiency is a crucial factor in algorithm design, as it determines how well an algorithm performs, especially when dealing with large datasets or time-sensitive tasks.

To evaluate the efficiency of an algorithm, computer scientists use the concept of time complexity. Time complexity measures how the running time of an algorithm grows as the size of the input data increases.

Algorithms with lower time complexity are more efficient, as they can handle larger inputs and complete tasks more quickly.

The concept of space complexity is also essential in algorithm analysis. Space complexity measures the amount of memory or storage space required by an algorithm as a function of the input size.

Efficient algorithms aim to minimize both time and space complexity, striking a balance between resource utilization and performance.

Algorithms are often categorized based on their specific problem-solving techniques. One common category is sorting algorithms, which rearrange a list of items into a specific order, such as ascending or descending.

Sorting algorithms play a fundamental role in various applications, from organizing data for efficient retrieval to facilitating data analysis and visualization.

Popular sorting algorithms include bubble sort, insertion sort, selection sort, merge sort, and quick sort, each with its own advantages and trade-offs in terms of time and space complexity.

Another category of algorithms is searching algorithms, which locate a specific item within a collection of data. Searching algorithms are essential in tasks like finding information on the internet, retrieving records from databases, and locating files on a computer.

Common searching algorithms include linear search, binary search, and hash-based search methods like hash tables.

In addition to sorting and searching, algorithms are used in problem-solving paradigms such as divide and conquer. Divide and conquer algorithms break down complex problems into smaller, more manageable subproblems, solve each subproblem independently, and then combine their solutions to solve the original problem.

The merge sort and quick sort algorithms are examples of divide and conquer techniques used for sorting.

Recursion is another fundamental concept in algorithm design. Recursion is a programming technique where a function calls itself to solve a problem.

Recursive algorithms are elegant and powerful but require careful design to ensure that they terminate and produce correct results.

The concept of data structures is closely related to algorithms. Data structures are ways of organizing and storing data efficiently, making it easier for algorithms to operate on that data.

Common data structures include arrays, linked lists, stacks, queues, trees, and graphs. Each data structure has its own characteristics and is suited to specific types of problems.

For example, arrays are efficient for random access to elements but may not be as flexible for inserting or deleting items. Linked lists, on the other hand, allow for efficient insertions and deletions but may require more memory.

Understanding the properties and trade-offs of different data structures is crucial for selecting the appropriate one for a particular algorithmic task.

The concept of algorithms extends beyond traditional computer science and is also applied in various interdisciplinary fields. For example, algorithms are used in computational biology to analyze DNA sequences, in operations research to optimize logistics and resource allocation, and in artificial intelligence for problem-solving and decision-making.

In summary, basic algorithmic concepts are the foundation of computer science and problem-solving. They provide a systematic approach to designing algorithms that are correct, efficient, and capable of solving a wide range of problems.

Whether you are a beginner learning the basics of algorithms or an experienced programmer tackling complex computational challenges, a solid understanding of these fundamental concepts is essential for success in the world of computing and technology.

Chapter 2: Building Blocks of Algorithm Design

Problem decomposition and abstraction are powerful techniques in computer science and problem-solving, enabling us to break down complex problems into more manageable parts. These techniques facilitate the development of efficient algorithms and the creation of software systems that can handle intricate tasks.

At its core, problem decomposition involves dividing a complex problem into smaller, more easily solvable subproblems. This process simplifies the overall problem-solving process and allows us to tackle each subproblem individually.

Consider a challenging task, such as designing an autonomous vehicle navigation system. This complex problem can be broken down into subproblems, including sensor data processing, path planning, obstacle avoidance, and control systems.

By decomposing the problem in this way, we can focus on solving each subproblem separately, making it easier to design and implement the entire navigation system.

Abstraction, on the other hand, involves simplifying the representation of a problem or system by ignoring irrelevant details. Abstraction allows us to focus on essential characteristics and properties while suppressing complexities that are not immediately relevant.

In the context of programming and software engineering, abstraction is a key concept. Programming languages provide various levels of abstraction, from low-level machine code to high-level languages like Python or Java.

High-level languages abstract away low-level details, such as memory management and hardware interactions, enabling programmers to concentrate on solving the problem at hand without getting bogged down in implementation details.

Abstraction also plays a crucial role in data modeling. Consider a database system used to store information about a library's book collection. Instead of storing every minute detail about each book, we abstract the data into relevant attributes like title, author, publication date, and ISBN.

This abstraction simplifies data storage, retrieval, and manipulation, making it more efficient and manageable.

Problem decomposition and abstraction often go hand in hand. Decomposing a problem into smaller subproblems can be viewed as a form of abstraction, as it allows us to focus on specific aspects of the problem while abstracting away the complexity of the whole.

In the field of algorithms and algorithmic design, these techniques are essential for developing efficient solutions to a wide range of problems. Let's explore how problem decomposition and abstraction are applied in algorithm development.

Sorting algorithms, for example, provide a compelling context for understanding problem decomposition and abstraction. The problem of sorting a list of items can be decomposed into subproblems related to comparing and rearranging elements.

One widely used sorting algorithm is merge sort, which employs a divide-and-conquer approach. In merge sort, the original list is divided into two smaller sublists, which are sorted independently.

The sorted sublists are then merged to produce the final sorted list. This decomposition of the sorting problem into smaller subproblems and the abstraction of each subproblem as a sorted sublist simplify the algorithm's design and analysis.

Another example of problem decomposition and abstraction is seen in graph algorithms. Graphs are mathematical structures that represent relationships between objects.

Graph algorithms, such as depth-first search (DFS) and breadth-first search (BFS), decompose the problem of traversing or analyzing a graph into smaller steps.

In DFS, the algorithm explores a path as deeply as possible before backtracking. This decomposition allows us to abstract the traversal process, making it easier to implement and analyze.

Similarly, the concept of abstraction is applied when designing data structures. Data structures like arrays, linked lists, trees, and hash tables abstract the underlying memory and organization of data, providing convenient ways to store and access information.

For example, an array abstracts the concept of a contiguous block of memory, allowing us to access elements by their indices. This abstraction simplifies the process of working with collections of data.

Problem decomposition and abstraction are also crucial in the design of computer networks and distributed systems. When building a large-scale network, engineers decompose the problem into subproblems like routing, addressing, and data transmission.

Each subproblem can be abstracted to focus on its specific requirements, enabling the design of efficient and scalable network architectures.

Abstraction plays a vital role in software engineering principles, such as object-oriented programming (OOP). In OOP, classes and objects are used to abstract complex real-world entities and their behaviors into manageable software components.

For instance, in a banking software system, you can create an abstract class "Account" that captures common attributes and operations for various types of bank accounts, such as savings accounts and checking accounts.

By abstracting these common elements into a single class, you simplify the design and maintenance of the software while promoting code reusability.

Problem decomposition and abstraction also find applications in artificial intelligence and machine learning. Machine learning models, for instance, abstract complex relationships in data by representing them as mathematical functions.

These functions can be decomposed into smaller components, such as layers in a neural network, each responsible for learning and abstracting specific features or patterns from the data.

In natural language processing, abstraction is used to extract essential information from text, ignoring irrelevant details. This abstraction enables machines to understand and process human language effectively.

In summary, problem decomposition and abstraction are fundamental techniques in computer science and problem-solving. They empower us to break down complex problems into manageable components, focus on essential aspects, and design efficient algorithms and software systems.

Whether you are designing algorithms, building software applications, or working on complex systems, these concepts are indispensable tools for tackling intricate computational challenges.

By mastering problem decomposition and abstraction, you can develop elegant and efficient solutions to a wide array of real-world problems, pushing the boundaries of what technology can achieve.

Algorithm design techniques are the strategies and methodologies that computer scientists and programmers employ to create effective and efficient algorithms for solving a wide range of problems. These techniques serve as guiding principles to streamline the process of algorithm development and optimization.

One of the foundational algorithm design techniques is brute force. Brute force involves solving a problem by systematically trying every possible solution until the correct one is found.

While brute force may be straightforward and guarantee a correct solution, it is often highly inefficient, especially for complex problems with a large search space.

Efficient algorithms, on the other hand, focus on minimizing the number of operations required to solve a problem. One common approach to achieving efficiency is through the use of data structures.

Data structures, such as arrays, linked lists, trees, and graphs, provide organized ways to store and manipulate data. Choosing the appropriate data structure for a problem can significantly impact the efficiency of the algorithm.

For instance, when searching for an element in a sorted array, a binary search algorithm is much more efficient than a linear search, which examines each element sequentially.

Another key algorithm design technique is divide and conquer. Divide and conquer algorithms break down a problem into smaller subproblems, solve each subproblem independently, and then combine their solutions to obtain the final result.

Merge sort and quick sort are classic examples of divide and conquer sorting algorithms that efficiently sort a list by repeatedly dividing it into smaller sublists, sorting each sublist, and then merging the sorted sublists back together.

Dynamic programming is another powerful algorithm design technique. It involves solving a problem by breaking it into overlapping subproblems and storing the results of each subproblem to avoid redundant calculations.

Dynamic programming is particularly useful for optimization problems where the goal is to find the best solution among many possible options.

A well-known example is the Fibonacci sequence, where dynamic programming can compute the nth Fibonacci number in linear time instead of exponential time using naive recursion.

Another fundamental technique is the greedy algorithm. Greedy algorithms make locally optimal choices at each step in the hope of finding a globally optimal solution.

While greedy algorithms are relatively simple to design and analyze, they may not always produce the best solution for every problem.

For example, the greedy coin change algorithm aims to find the minimum number of coins needed to make change for a given amount. It chooses the largest denomination coin at each step until the target amount is reached.

However, this approach doesn't guarantee the minimum number of coins for all coin denominations.

Backtracking is an algorithmic technique that involves exploring all possible solutions to a problem by systematically trying different options and undoing them when necessary.

Backtracking is commonly used in solving problems like Sudoku puzzles, the traveling salesman problem, and maze solving.

Branch and bound is an algorithm design technique that combines elements of both divide and conquer and backtracking. It efficiently explores the solution space of combinatorial optimization problems while eliminating branches that cannot yield a better solution than the current best-known solution.

This technique is often applied to problems such as the traveling salesman problem and the knapsack problem.

Randomized algorithms introduce an element of randomness into the algorithm's behavior. These algorithms can be particularly useful for problems where finding an exact solution is computationally infeasible or where approximate solutions are acceptable.

One well-known randomized algorithm is the Monte Carlo method, used for estimating numerical results through random sampling.

Las Vegas algorithms, on the other hand, always produce the correct answer, but their running time may vary depending on the input.

Simulated annealing, a probabilistic optimization technique, is an example of a Las Vegas algorithm that is used for finding approximate solutions to optimization problems.

Heuristic algorithms are another class of algorithms that provide approximate solutions to optimization problems. Heuristics are problem-solving techniques that use a rule of thumb or a "best guess" approach to quickly find a solution that is often good enough for practical purposes.

Ant colony optimization and genetic algorithms are heuristic techniques commonly applied to optimization problems in various fields, including logistics, scheduling, and engineering design.

Metaheuristic algorithms, such as genetic algorithms, simulated annealing, and particle swarm optimization, provide general-purpose optimization techniques that can be applied to a wide range of problems.

These algorithms often draw inspiration from natural processes, such as evolution, to find near-optimal solutions in complex search spaces.

In addition to these algorithm design techniques, parallel and distributed algorithms are essential in the era of multi-core processors and distributed computing environments.

Parallel algorithms divide a problem into smaller tasks that can be executed simultaneously on multiple processors or cores, aiming to achieve improved performance and reduced execution time.

Distributed algorithms address problems that involve multiple interconnected systems or nodes, where coordination and communication between nodes are critical.

Graph algorithms, which focus on analyzing and manipulating graphs or networks, are prevalent in various applications, including social network analysis, network routing, and recommendation systems.

These algorithms deal with tasks like finding the shortest path, detecting cycles, and discovering communities in networks.

Algorithm design techniques are not limited to theoretical concepts but have practical implications in diverse domains, from computer science and operations research to artificial intelligence and machine learning.

Understanding these techniques and their trade-offs is essential for computer scientists and engineers seeking to develop efficient and effective algorithms for real-world problems.

Moreover, the selection of the appropriate algorithm design technique depends on the problem's nature, constraints, and objectives, highlighting the importance of algorithmic thinking and problem-solving skills in the field of computer science and beyond.

Chapter 3: Algorithm Efficiency and Analysis

Time and space complexity analysis is a crucial aspect of algorithm design and evaluation, providing insights into an algorithm's efficiency and resource utilization. By understanding these complexities, we can make informed decisions about algorithm selection, optimization, and scalability.

Time complexity measures how the running time of an algorithm grows as a function of the input size. It quantifies the number of basic operations, or steps, performed by the algorithm relative to the size of the input.

To analyze time complexity, we often use Big O notation, which provides an upper bound on the growth rate of an algorithm's running time. For example, an algorithm with a time complexity of $O(n)$ implies that its running time increases linearly with the input size.

The concept of asymptotic analysis is central to time complexity analysis. It focuses on the behavior of algorithms as the input size approaches infinity, rather than precise measurements for specific inputs.

Common time complexities include $O(1)$ for constant time algorithms, $O(\log n)$ for algorithms with logarithmic time complexity, $O(n)$ for linear time algorithms, and $O(n^2)$ for quadratic time algorithms.

Higher time complexities like $O(2^n)$ indicate exponential growth, which can become prohibitively slow for large inputs.

Space complexity, on the other hand, measures the amount of memory or storage space required by an algorithm as a function of the input size. It is essential for understanding how an algorithm's memory usage scales with input growth.

Similar to time complexity, space complexity can also be analyzed using Big O notation. For example, an algorithm with a space complexity of O(1) indicates constant memory usage, while O(n) signifies linear space usage relative to the input size.

Space complexity analysis considers both auxiliary space, which includes memory for variables and data structures, and input space, which accounts for the memory required to store the input.

Balancing time and space complexity is a critical aspect of algorithm design. Efficient algorithms aim to minimize both time and space complexity, striking a balance between computational resource utilization and performance.

In some cases, algorithms trade time for space or vice versa, depending on the specific requirements of the problem. This trade-off is known as the time-space trade-off.

Time and space complexity analysis is often performed through worst-case, average-case, and best-case scenarios. The worst-case scenario provides an upper bound on the algorithm's performance, considering the input that results in the maximum number of operations or memory usage.

The best-case scenario represents the algorithm's behavior when given the input that results in the fewest operations or minimal memory usage. The average-case scenario considers the expected performance across a range of inputs, accounting for their likelihood of occurrence.

Analyzing worst-case complexity is particularly important for real-time systems or critical applications where performance guarantees are essential.

The big O notation categorizes algorithms into complexity classes, helping us classify and compare their efficiency. Common complexity classes include constant time (O(1)), logarithmic time (O(log n)), linear time (O(n)), linearithmic time (O(n log n)), quadratic time (O(n^2)), and exponential time (O(2^n)).

Linear time algorithms are generally considered efficient and are commonly used in practice. Linearithmic time algorithms, such as those used in efficient sorting and searching, are also prevalent.

Quadratic and exponential time algorithms are less efficient and may only be suitable for small inputs or special cases.

Time complexity analysis helps us make informed decisions when choosing algorithms for specific tasks. For example, when dealing with large datasets, selecting an O(n log n) sorting algorithm like merge sort or quicksort is more practical than an O(n^2) algorithm like bubble sort.

Efficient algorithms often use data structures to optimize operations. For instance, hash tables provide constant-time average-case performance for inserting, deleting, and retrieving elements, making them suitable for fast data access.

Balancing time and space complexity is crucial for designing algorithms that meet performance and memory requirements. In some cases, algorithms can be adapted to use less memory at the cost of increased computation time or vice versa.

Algorithmic optimization techniques, such as memoization in dynamic programming or pruning in search algorithms, aim to reduce time and space complexity by eliminating redundant calculations or exploring fewer possibilities.

The choice of data structures also plays a significant role in space complexity. Efficient data structures can minimize memory usage and improve overall algorithm performance.

Analyzing and understanding time and space complexity are valuable skills for computer scientists and programmers. These skills allow us to design efficient algorithms, optimize existing ones, and make informed decisions when selecting algorithms for specific tasks.

Moreover, time and space complexity analysis is essential for evaluating algorithm scalability, predicting their behavior under varying input sizes, and ensuring that they meet the performance requirements of real-world applications.

While algorithmic efficiency is crucial, it is also important to consider trade-offs, as optimizing one aspect may lead to compromises in another. Overall, time and space complexity analysis is a cornerstone of algorithm design and a fundamental skill for anyone working in the field of computer science and software development.

Asymptotic notation is a fundamental tool in the analysis of algorithms and their efficiency, allowing us to describe how an algorithm's performance scales as the input size grows. It provides a concise and abstract representation of an algorithm's time and space complexity, focusing on its behavior as the input approaches infinity.

One of the most commonly used forms of asymptotic notation is Big O notation, denoted as $O(f(n))$, where "f(n)" represents a mathematical function of the input size "n." Big O notation provides an upper bound on the growth rate of an algorithm's resource usage, typically in terms of time or space.

For example, if an algorithm has a time complexity of $O(n)$, it implies that the number of basic operations it performs is linearly proportional to the input size. As the input size increases, the running time of the algorithm grows at a rate no faster than a linear function of the input.

This abstraction is powerful because it allows us to classify algorithms into complexity classes and make comparisons between them without getting bogged down in the details of specific implementations or constant factors.

Another commonly used asymptotic notation is Omega notation, denoted as $\Omega(f(n))$. Omega notation provides a lower bound on the growth rate of an algorithm's resource usage.

For instance, if an algorithm has a time complexity of $\Omega(n^2)$, it means that the algorithm's running time must grow at least as quickly as a quadratic function of the input size.

Finally, Theta notation, denoted as $\Theta(f(n))$, provides a tight bound on the growth rate of an algorithm's resource usage. If an algorithm has a time complexity of $\Theta(f(n))$, it means that the algorithm's running time grows at the same rate as the function $f(n)$ for all input sizes, up to constant factors.

In practice, Big O notation is the most commonly used form of asymptotic notation, as it describes the upper bound on an algorithm's performance, which is often the most relevant information when comparing and selecting algorithms.

Efficiency in the context of algorithm analysis refers to how well an algorithm utilizes computational resources such as time and space. Efficient algorithms are designed to perform their tasks with minimal resource consumption, making them suitable for a wide range of practical applications.

Efficiency is a critical consideration when designing algorithms because it directly impacts the algorithm's usability and performance. In many cases, it can be the difference between a feasible solution and one that is too slow or resource-intensive to be practical.

When analyzing algorithm efficiency, we often focus on two primary aspects: time complexity and space complexity. Time complexity measures how the running time of an algorithm scales with the input size, while space complexity quantifies the algorithm's memory usage in a similar manner.

Efficient algorithms aim to achieve low time and space complexities, meaning they can handle large inputs or perform tasks quickly without excessive memory consumption.

To illustrate the importance of efficiency, consider a sorting algorithm. Sorting is a fundamental operation in computer science and has applications in various fields, from databases and search engines to data analysis and information retrieval.

An efficient sorting algorithm, such as merge sort or quicksort with a time complexity of $O(n \log n)$, can efficiently sort large datasets. In contrast, an inefficient sorting algorithm, like bubble sort with a time complexity of $O(n^2)$, may struggle with large inputs and lead to significant delays.

Efficiency is not only relevant to time complexity but also to space complexity. Space-efficient algorithms can process data without requiring excessive memory, making them suitable for applications with limited memory resources.

For example, consider an algorithm used in image processing. Efficient image processing algorithms can manipulate large images without consuming excessive memory, allowing them to run on devices with limited RAM.

The choice of algorithm can significantly impact the efficiency of a software system. In real-world scenarios, it's common to encounter large datasets, complex computations, and resource constraints.

Efficient algorithms can make the difference between a responsive and reliable system and one that struggles to perform even basic tasks.

When analyzing efficiency, it's essential to consider both worst-case and average-case scenarios. The worst-case scenario represents the algorithm's performance when given the input that results in the maximum resource usage.

Analyzing the worst-case scenario is crucial for ensuring that the algorithm can handle the most challenging inputs without running into performance issues.

On the other hand, the average-case scenario provides insights into the algorithm's typical performance. It considers the distribution of inputs that the algorithm is likely to encounter in practice.

Efficiency considerations are particularly important in fields such as artificial intelligence and machine learning. These fields often involve processing vast amounts of data and performing complex computations.

Efficient algorithms are crucial for training machine learning models, optimizing neural networks, and solving large-scale optimization problems.

Moreover, the efficiency of algorithms is critical in areas like cryptography and cybersecurity, where the ability to perform fast and secure computations is paramount.

In summary, asymptotic notation and efficiency analysis play a central role in algorithm design and evaluation. They allow us to abstractly quantify an algorithm's performance, making it easier to compare, select, and optimize algorithms for a wide range of applications.

Efficient algorithms are essential for handling real-world challenges, where large inputs, resource constraints, and performance requirements are common.

By understanding asymptotic notation and considering efficiency during algorithm design, computer scientists and programmers can create solutions that are not only correct but also practical and scalable.

Chapter 4: Sorting and Searching Techniques

Sorting algorithms are fundamental techniques used in computer science and data processing to arrange a collection of items in a specific order. These algorithms play a vital role in various applications, from organizing data for efficient searching and retrieval to facilitating tasks like ranking and data analysis.

Sorting is a common operation in everyday life, such as organizing a list of names alphabetically or arranging a deck of playing cards. In computer science, sorting is a foundational problem with numerous algorithms developed over the years to tackle it efficiently.

One of the simplest sorting algorithms is the bubble sort. Bubble sort repeatedly compares adjacent elements in a list and swaps them if they are in the wrong order. This process continues until the entire list is sorted.

Although bubble sort is easy to understand and implement, it has a time complexity of $O(n^2)$, making it inefficient for large datasets.

Insertion sort is another elementary sorting algorithm. It works by repeatedly taking an element from the unsorted portion of the list and inserting it into the correct position within the sorted portion. Insertion sort also has a time complexity of $O(n^2)$.

Selection sort is yet another basic sorting algorithm. It repeatedly selects the smallest (or largest) element from the unsorted portion of the list and places it in the sorted portion. Like bubble and insertion sort, its time complexity is $O(n^2)$.

While these sorting algorithms are straightforward and useful for small datasets, they become impractical for larger inputs due to their quadratic time complexity.

To improve sorting efficiency, more advanced algorithms like merge sort and quicksort were developed. Merge sort is a divide-and-conquer algorithm that splits the list into smaller sublists, recursively sorts them, and then merges them together. It has a time complexity of $O(n \log n)$, making it significantly faster than quadratic-time algorithms.

Quicksort, on the other hand, is a divide-and-conquer algorithm that selects a "pivot" element, partitions the list into elements smaller and larger than the pivot, and recursively sorts the sublists. Quicksort's average-case time complexity is $O(n \log n)$, but it can degrade to $O(n^2)$ in the worst case.

Heap sort is another efficient sorting algorithm that uses a binary heap data structure. It first builds a max-heap (or min-heap), repeatedly extracts the maximum (or minimum) element, and places it in the sorted portion of the list. Heap sort has a time complexity of $O(n \log n)$ and is particularly useful when a stable sort is not required.

In addition to the comparison-based sorting algorithms mentioned above, there are non-comparison-based sorting algorithms like counting sort and radix sort. These algorithms exploit specific characteristics of the data to achieve linear time complexity, making them exceptionally fast for certain scenarios.

Counting sort, for example, counts the number of occurrences of each element in the input and uses this information to place elements in their correct sorted positions. It has a time complexity of $O(n + k)$, where "k" is the range of possible values in the input, making it efficient when "k" is small compared to the input size.

Radix sort, on the other hand, sorts elements by considering their digits or characters one at a time, from the least significant to the most significant. This approach can be particularly efficient for sorting integers or strings and has a time complexity of $O(kn)$, where "k" is the number of digits or characters.

Sorting algorithms can be categorized as either in-place or not in-place. In-place sorting algorithms rearrange elements within the existing data structure, using a constant amount of additional memory. Examples of in-place sorting algorithms include insertion sort, selection sort, and in-place quicksort.

Non in-place sorting algorithms, on the other hand, require additional memory to store temporary data structures. Merge sort, for instance, creates new sublists during the merge phase, necessitating additional memory.

Stability is another characteristic of sorting algorithms. A stable sort preserves the relative order of equal elements in the sorted list. For example, if two records have the same key, a stable sort ensures that their original order is maintained.

Some sorting algorithms, like bubble sort and insertion sort, are naturally stable, while others, like quicksort, can be modified to achieve stability.

The choice of a sorting algorithm depends on several factors, including the size of the dataset, the presence of duplicate elements, memory constraints, and the need for a stable sort.

In practice, many programming languages and libraries provide built-in sorting functions that offer a good balance of time and space complexity for general use cases. These sorting functions are often highly optimized and efficient.

Sorting algorithms continue to be a rich area of study in computer science, with ongoing research focusing on further improving their efficiency and adaptability to various data types and application domains.

In summary, sorting algorithms are essential tools in computer science and data processing, enabling us to efficiently organize and analyze data. They come in various flavors, each with its strengths and weaknesses, making them suitable for different scenarios and requirements.

Understanding the characteristics and trade-offs of different sorting algorithms is crucial for selecting the most appropriate one for a particular task, ultimately contributing to the efficiency and effectiveness of software systems.

Efficient searching methods are fundamental in computer science and data analysis, enabling us to quickly locate specific items or information within large datasets. Whether you're searching for a particular record in a database, finding a specific word in a document, or looking for a friend's profile on a social media platform, efficient searching methods play a crucial role in ensuring a fast and responsive user experience.

One of the simplest and most widely used searching methods is linear search. Linear search, also known as sequential search, involves scanning through a list of items one by one until the desired item is found or the entire list is checked.

While linear search is straightforward to implement, it has a time complexity of $O(n)$, where "n" is the number of items in the list. This means that in the worst case, it may require checking every item in the list, making it inefficient for large datasets.

To improve search efficiency, binary search is a commonly employed method. Binary search is particularly effective for sorted lists or arrays. It works by repeatedly dividing the search interval in half and comparing the middle element to the target value.

If the middle element is equal to the target value, the search is successful. Otherwise, the search continues in the appropriate subinterval, reducing the search space by half with each iteration.

Binary search has a time complexity of O(log n), making it significantly faster than linear search for large datasets. This efficiency stems from its ability to eliminate half of the remaining items in each iteration.

Binary search is a divide-and-conquer algorithm that exploits the properties of sorted data to achieve a substantial reduction in the number of comparisons required to find the target value.

Interpolation search is another searching method suitable for sorted datasets. Unlike binary search, which always examines the middle element, interpolation search estimates the likely position of the target value based on its value and the range of values in the dataset.

By making an educated guess about the target's position, interpolation search can potentially outperform binary search when the data is distributed unevenly.

Hashing is a technique used in computer science to implement efficient data retrieval. It involves mapping keys or values to specific locations in a data structure, such as an array, using a hash function.

A hash function takes an input value, typically a key, and produces a fixed-size hash code. This hash code is used to determine the storage location, or "bucket," in which the corresponding data is stored.

Hashing allows for constant-time average-case search, insertion, and deletion operations when the hash function distributes the data evenly across the available buckets.

Common data structures that use hashing for efficient searching include hash tables and hash maps. These data structures are widely used in databases, caching mechanisms, and data storage systems.

In addition to the methods mentioned above, tree-based searching algorithms, such as binary search trees (BSTs), are powerful tools for efficient data retrieval.

A binary search tree is a hierarchical data structure where each node has two child nodes, typically organized such that values less than the node's value are in its left subtree, and values greater than the node's value are in its right subtree.

Searching in a balanced binary search tree, such as an AVL tree or a red-black tree, has a time complexity of $O(\log n)$ on average. This makes tree-based searching methods suitable for datasets that need to maintain a sorted order.

However, it's important to note that the efficiency of tree-based searching depends on the balance of the tree. An unbalanced tree can lead to worst-case time complexities of $O(n)$, where "n" is the number of elements in the tree.

In practice, various advanced searching techniques and data structures have been developed to address specific search requirements and constraints.

For example, the B-tree is a self-balancing tree structure optimized for disk storage, commonly used in databases and file systems.

Trie structures are used for efficient string matching and retrieval, making them suitable for applications like text indexing and autocomplete.

Spatial indexing methods, such as R-trees and Quad-trees, are employed in geographic information systems (GIS) to efficiently search for spatial objects like points, lines, and polygons.

When dealing with unstructured or semi-structured data, full-text search engines like Elasticsearch and Apache Lucene provide powerful and efficient searching capabilities, including features like relevance ranking and text analysis.

Efficient searching is not limited to one-dimensional data. In multidimensional data, spatial indexing methods like KD-trees and R*-trees are used to efficiently search for data points in multiple dimensions, such as geographic coordinates or feature vectors.

Efficiency in searching methods is often a trade-off between various factors, including time complexity, space complexity, and the specific requirements of the application. Different searching methods are chosen based on the nature of the data, the expected query patterns, and the available computational resources.

Efficient searching methods continue to be a vibrant area of research, with ongoing efforts to develop new algorithms and data structures that address the evolving needs of modern computing and data analysis.

In summary, efficient searching methods are essential tools in computer science and data processing, allowing us to quickly locate specific information within large datasets. From linear search to advanced data structures and algorithms, the choice of a searching method depends on the nature of the data and the specific requirements of the application.

Understanding the strengths and weaknesses of different searching methods is crucial for designing and implementing systems that provide fast and responsive search functionality, enhancing user experiences and enabling efficient data retrieval and analysis.

Chapter 5: Dynamic Programming and Greedy Algorithms

Dynamic programming is a powerful and versatile technique used in computer science and mathematics to solve complex problems by breaking them down into simpler subproblems. It is a problem-solving approach that can significantly improve the efficiency of algorithms by avoiding redundant computations and storing intermediate results for reuse.

At its core, dynamic programming relies on the principle of solving a problem by combining solutions to its subproblems. By breaking down a complex problem into smaller, more manageable parts and solving each part only once, dynamic programming can achieve impressive time and space savings.

One of the key features of dynamic programming is memoization, which involves storing the results of expensive function calls and returning the cached result when the same inputs occur again. This caching mechanism eliminates the need to recompute solutions for subproblems that have already been solved, reducing time complexity.

Dynamic programming is particularly effective when dealing with optimization problems, where the goal is to find the best solution among a set of possible solutions. Examples of optimization problems include finding the shortest path in a graph, maximizing profit in a resource allocation problem, or minimizing the cost of a sequence of actions.

Dynamic programming can be applied to a wide range of domains and problem types. It is commonly used in computer science, operations research, artificial intelligence, and economics, among others.

A classic example of dynamic programming is the Fibonacci sequence. In this sequence, each number is the sum of the two preceding ones: 0, 1, 1, 2, 3, 5, 8, 13, 21, and so on.

A straightforward recursive approach to calculating Fibonacci numbers would involve repeatedly calling the function with smaller input values, but this leads to exponential time complexity.

By using dynamic programming with memoization, we can compute Fibonacci numbers efficiently. The algorithm stores the results of previously computed Fibonacci numbers and reuses them to calculate larger ones, reducing the number of recursive calls and achieving linear time complexity.

Dynamic programming can be categorized into two main approaches: top-down and bottom-up. Top-down dynamic programming starts with the original problem and recursively breaks it down into smaller subproblems, solving them along the way.

Bottom-up dynamic programming, on the other hand, starts with the simplest subproblems and builds up to the original problem. It typically involves using iterative loops to compute solutions for increasingly complex subproblems, avoiding the overhead of function calls.

The choice between top-down and bottom-up dynamic programming depends on the problem and personal preference. Some programmers prefer the clarity and simplicity of top-down recursion, while others favor the efficiency and optimization potential of bottom-up iteration.

An important concept in dynamic programming is the concept of overlapping subproblems. These are subproblems that recur multiple times during the solution of a larger problem. Dynamic programming leverages the fact that solutions to overlapping subproblems can be reused to reduce computational overhead.

To identify and address overlapping subproblems, dynamic programming often employs techniques like memoization tables or arrays. These data structures store intermediate results, allowing the algorithm to look up and reuse solutions for previously encountered subproblems.

Another key concept in dynamic programming is the principle of optimal substructure. This property means that the optimal solution to a larger problem can be constructed from optimal solutions to its subproblems.

In essence, dynamic programming breaks a problem down into subproblems, solves them optimally, and then combines their solutions to find the optimal solution to the original problem.

The dynamic programming paradigm is applicable to various problem-solving techniques, including divide and conquer, greedy algorithms, and backtracking. It can be used to solve problems in diverse domains, such as shortest path algorithms, text and string processing, image processing, and more.

One famous dynamic programming algorithm is Dijkstra's algorithm for finding the shortest path in a weighted graph. It efficiently computes the shortest distances from a source node to all other nodes, making it widely used in routing and network optimization.

Another classic example is the knapsack problem, a combinatorial optimization problem. Dynamic programming can be employed to determine the optimal selection of items with given weights and values, maximizing the value within a weight constraint.

In addition to these well-known examples, dynamic programming can be applied to various other problems, from DNA sequence alignment to resource scheduling and from image recognition to machine learning.

Dynamic programming is not a one-size-fits-all solution. While it is a powerful technique, it may not be the best choice for every problem. In some cases, the overhead of maintaining memoization tables or arrays may outweigh the benefits of optimization.

Furthermore, dynamic programming often requires careful analysis of the problem's structure to identify subproblems and establish their relationships. The ability to decompose a problem into subproblems and define their optimal substructure is essential for successfully applying dynamic programming.

Despite its challenges, dynamic programming is a valuable tool in a programmer's arsenal. It can lead to elegant and efficient solutions for complex problems, and its principles can be adapted to various problem domains.

The key to mastering dynamic programming lies in practice and understanding the core concepts of memoization, overlapping subproblems, and optimal substructure.

By applying dynamic programming principles effectively, programmers can tackle a wide range of problems with confidence, ultimately leading to more efficient and optimized solutions in both software development and algorithm design.

Greedy algorithms are a class of algorithms that follow the "greedy" strategy of making the locally optimal choice at each step with the hope of finding a global optimum. This means that at each step of the algorithm, it selects the best available option without considering the consequences of that choice on future steps.

The primary advantage of greedy algorithms is their simplicity and efficiency. They often require minimal computational resources and are relatively easy to implement.

However, the drawback of greedy algorithms is that they do not guarantee finding the globally optimal solution. In some cases, a greedy algorithm may produce a suboptimal solution that is not the best possible outcome.

Despite this limitation, greedy algorithms are widely used in various domains, including optimization problems, scheduling, and resource allocation, where the locally optimal choice often leads to an acceptable or near-optimal solution.

One classic example of a greedy algorithm is the coin change problem. Given a set of coin denominations and a target amount, the goal is to make change for the target amount using the fewest possible coins.

The greedy strategy for this problem involves repeatedly selecting the largest coin denomination that is less than or equal to the remaining change until the target amount is reached.

While the greedy algorithm works well for standard coin systems, such as the U.S. coin system (penny, nickel, dime, quarter), it may not produce an optimal solution for arbitrary coin denominations.

For example, if the coin denominations are {1, 3, 4} and the target amount is 6, the greedy algorithm would produce a suboptimal solution of {4, 1, 1}, requiring three coins instead of the optimal solution {3, 3}, which requires only two coins.

This example illustrates the importance of carefully analyzing the problem's characteristics and the suitability of the greedy strategy.

Another classic application of greedy algorithms is in the realm of scheduling. The interval scheduling problem involves selecting a maximum-sized subset of non-overlapping intervals from a set of intervals.

The greedy strategy for this problem is to select intervals based on their finish times. At each step, choose the interval with the earliest finish time that does not overlap with previously selected intervals.

This greedy approach ensures that the selected subset of intervals is both non-overlapping and maximizes the number of intervals included.

Greedy algorithms also find application in various network and routing problems. One well-known example is Dijkstra's algorithm for finding the shortest path in a weighted graph.

Dijkstra's algorithm starts from a source node and explores neighboring nodes in increasing order of their distance from the source. It maintains a set of visited nodes and continually selects the unvisited node with the shortest path from the source.

This process repeats until all nodes have been visited or the target node is reached, guaranteeing the discovery of the shortest path in a graph with non-negative edge weights.

However, Dijkstra's algorithm may not produce correct results in graphs with negative edge weights, as it assumes that the shortest path has already been found for any visited node.

In such cases, the Bellman-Ford algorithm is a more suitable choice, as it can handle graphs with negative edge weights and detect the presence of negative cycles.

Greedy algorithms can also be applied to problems involving minimum spanning trees. The minimum spanning tree is a subgraph that includes all vertices of a connected graph while minimizing the total edge weight.

One commonly used algorithm for this purpose is Kruskal's algorithm. Kruskal's algorithm starts with an empty set of edges and repeatedly adds the edge with the smallest weight that does not create a cycle until a minimum spanning tree is formed.

Another approach is Prim's algorithm, which starts with a single vertex and adds vertices and edges incrementally to build the minimum spanning tree.

While greedy algorithms can be effective in solving a wide range of problems, it is important to recognize their limitations. In some cases, a more comprehensive exploration of solution space, such as through dynamic programming or backtracking, may be required to guarantee the optimal solution.

Additionally, the choice of a greedy algorithm should align with the problem's characteristics and constraints. Understanding the problem's structure and the potential consequences of the greedy choices made at each step is crucial for the successful application of these algorithms.

In summary, greedy algorithms are a class of algorithms that make locally optimal choices at each step in the hope of finding a global optimum. They are simple and efficient but do not guarantee the best possible solution in all cases.

Greedy strategies find applications in various domains, including coin change problems, interval scheduling, shortest path algorithms, and minimum spanning trees.

However, their suitability and correctness depend on the problem's characteristics, and careful analysis is essential to determine when and how to apply greedy algorithms effectively.

Chapter 6: Graph Algorithms: Traversals and Shortest Paths

Graph traversal algorithms are fundamental techniques used in computer science to explore and navigate the nodes and edges of a graph. They play a crucial role in various applications, such as network routing, social network analysis, recommendation systems, and pathfinding in video games.

One of the simplest graph traversal algorithms is depth-first search (DFS). DFS starts at an initial node and explores as far as possible along each branch before backtracking. This process continues until all nodes have been visited.

DFS can be implemented using recursion or a stack data structure. The algorithm is particularly useful for exploring paths and detecting cycles in a graph.

However, DFS does not guarantee the shortest path in a weighted graph and may not find the optimal solution in all cases.

Breadth-first search (BFS) is another fundamental graph traversal algorithm. BFS explores all the neighbor nodes at the current level before moving on to the next level. This approach ensures that the shortest path to each reachable node is discovered first.

BFS uses a queue data structure to keep track of the nodes to be visited next. It is commonly used for finding the shortest path in an unweighted graph and can also be used for tasks like web crawling and network discovery.

Both DFS and BFS are uninformed search algorithms, meaning they do not use any additional information about the graph to guide their exploration.

In contrast, informed search algorithms, like Dijkstra's algorithm and the A* algorithm, take advantage of additional information, such as edge weights or heuristic estimates, to make more informed decisions during traversal.

Dijkstra's algorithm is used to find the shortest path from a single source node to all other nodes in a weighted graph. It maintains a priority queue of nodes to be explored and continually selects the node with the shortest known distance from the source.

Dijkstra's algorithm guarantees the shortest path in non-negative weighted graphs but may not work correctly in the presence of negative edge weights.

The A* algorithm is a heuristic search algorithm that combines the benefits of BFS and Dijkstra's algorithm. It uses a heuristic function to estimate the cost from the current node to the goal node, guiding the search towards the goal.

A* is widely used in pathfinding problems, such as finding routes in GPS navigation systems and video games. It can be customized by choosing different heuristic functions to balance exploration speed and solution quality.

In addition to these traversal algorithms, there are more specialized algorithms for specific graph types and tasks.

For example, topological sorting is used to order nodes in a directed acyclic graph (DAG) such that every directed edge goes from earlier to later in the order. Topological sorting is essential for tasks like scheduling and dependency resolution.

Kruskal's algorithm and Prim's algorithm are used to find the minimum spanning tree of a connected, undirected graph. They are commonly used in network design and optimization problems.

Graph traversal algorithms also play a significant role in social network analysis. They are used to find influential nodes, identify communities, and analyze the spread of information or diseases in networks.

In recommendation systems, graph traversal algorithms can be used to discover relationships between users and items, enabling personalized recommendations.

The efficient implementation of graph traversal algorithms depends on the data structures used to represent the graph. Common representations include adjacency matrices and adjacency lists.

An adjacency matrix is a two-dimensional array where each cell represents the presence or absence of an edge between two nodes. It is suitable for dense graphs but can be inefficient for sparse graphs due to its high memory usage.

An adjacency list is a data structure that stores a list of neighbors for each node. It is more memory-efficient for sparse graphs and is commonly used in practice.

Graph traversal algorithms can also be adapted for parallel and distributed computing, making them suitable for analyzing large-scale networks and data.

In summary, graph traversal algorithms are essential tools in computer science and have a wide range of applications. DFS and BFS are fundamental for exploring graphs, while Dijkstra's algorithm and A* are used for finding shortest paths.

Specialized algorithms like topological sorting, Kruskal's algorithm, and Prim's algorithm cater to specific graph types and tasks.

The choice of algorithm depends on the nature of the graph and the problem at hand, and efficient implementation relies on appropriate data structures and optimization techniques.

Understanding and mastering these algorithms is essential for solving graph-related problems and building intelligent systems that leverage the rich structure of interconnected data.

Shortest path algorithms are a fundamental part of graph theory and network analysis, focusing on finding the most efficient path between two points in a graph. These algorithms are widely used in various applications, including routing in computer networks, navigation systems, logistics optimization, and even social network analysis.

One of the most well-known and widely used shortest path algorithms is Dijkstra's algorithm. Dijkstra's algorithm finds the shortest path from a specified source node to all other nodes in a weighted graph.

The algorithm maintains a set of visited nodes and a set of unvisited nodes. It starts by assigning a tentative distance value to every node, with the source node having a distance of zero and all other nodes initially set to infinity.

At each step, the algorithm selects the unvisited node with the smallest tentative distance and considers all of its neighbors. It calculates the sum of the tentative distance to the selected node and the weight of the edge to its neighbor.

If this sum is less than the neighbor's current tentative distance, the algorithm updates the neighbor's distance with the new, shorter distance. This process continues until all nodes have been visited or the target node is reached.

Dijkstra's algorithm guarantees the shortest path in graphs with non-negative edge weights. It produces accurate results and is relatively easy to implement.

However, it is not suitable for graphs with negative edge weights, as it assumes that the shortest path has already been found for any visited node. Negative edge weights can lead to incorrect results and infinite loops in the algorithm.

To handle graphs with negative edge weights and detect the presence of negative cycles, the Bellman-Ford algorithm is a more appropriate choice. The Bellman-Ford algorithm iteratively relaxes the edges of the graph, updating distance estimates until convergence.

In the presence of negative cycles, the algorithm detects them by observing that distance estimates continue to decrease in subsequent iterations. This detection capability makes Bellman-Ford suitable for scenarios where the graph may contain negative cycles, such as modeling financial transactions or airline routes.

Another commonly used shortest path algorithm is the A* algorithm. A* combines elements of both Dijkstra's algorithm and greedy search. It uses a heuristic function to estimate the cost from the current node to the goal node, guiding the search toward the goal.

A* maintains a priority queue of nodes to be explored, selecting nodes based on a combination of their tentative distance from the source and the heuristic estimate to the goal. This approach ensures that the algorithm explores promising paths first, often leading to more efficient searches than pure breadth-first or Dijkstra's algorithms.

The choice of heuristic function in A* can significantly impact the algorithm's performance. A good heuristic should provide a meaningful estimate of the remaining cost while ensuring that A* retains its admissibility and consistency properties.

Admissibility means that the heuristic never overestimates the actual cost to reach the goal. Consistency ensures that the heuristic follows a triangle inequality, where the estimated cost from the current node to the goal is less than or equal to the sum of the estimated cost from the current node to a neighbor and the estimated cost from that neighbor to the goal.

A* is commonly used in pathfinding problems, such as finding routes in GPS navigation systems and video games. By selecting a suitable heuristic and combining it with the right data structures, A* can efficiently find the shortest path in large graphs.

Aside from these classical shortest path algorithms, variations and optimizations exist to address specific scenarios. For example, if the graph is sparse and only a single shortest path is needed, a bidirectional search can be employed to search from both the source and target nodes simultaneously.

In grid-based pathfinding, where the graph represents a grid of cells, algorithms like the A* algorithm are often augmented with additional optimizations like jump point search (JPS) to reduce the number of nodes explored.

In summary, shortest path algorithms are essential tools in computer science and network analysis. Dijkstra's algorithm, Bellman-Ford, and A* are among the most commonly used algorithms for finding the shortest path in graphs.

The choice of algorithm depends on the problem's characteristics and requirements, such as the presence of negative edge weights or the need for a heuristic-guided search.

By understanding the principles and trade-offs of these algorithms, practitioners can efficiently solve a wide range of routing and optimization problems in diverse domains, ultimately improving efficiency and resource allocation in various applications.

Chapter 7: Divide and Conquer Strategies

Divide and conquer is a fundamental problem-solving technique used in computer science and mathematics. The essence of divide and conquer is to break down a complex problem into smaller, more manageable subproblems, solve these subproblems independently, and then combine their solutions to solve the original problem.

The divide and conquer strategy can be applied to a wide range of problems, from sorting and searching algorithms to computational geometry and dynamic programming.

The basic idea behind divide and conquer is to divide the problem into smaller instances that are similar to the original problem but simpler to solve. These smaller instances are often referred to as subproblems.

Once the problem has been divided into subproblems, the next step is to conquer each subproblem. This means solving each subproblem independently to find its solution.

The final step of the divide and conquer approach is to combine the solutions of the subproblems to obtain the solution of the original problem. This step is often referred to as the merge or combine step.

The divide and conquer strategy is particularly useful for solving problems that can be broken down into smaller, independent parts. It is a powerful technique for solving problems efficiently and can lead to algorithms with better time complexity compared to other approaches.

One of the classic examples of a divide and conquer algorithm is the merge sort algorithm. Merge sort is used to sort a list of elements by dividing it into smaller sublists, sorting each sublist, and then merging the sorted sublists to obtain the final sorted list.

The merge sort algorithm starts by dividing the input list into two equal-sized sublists. Each sublist is then sorted recursively using the same merge sort algorithm.

Once the sublists are sorted, the merge step combines them to create a single sorted list. This merge step is what makes merge sort a divide and conquer algorithm.

Merge sort is known for its stable sorting property, which means that equal elements maintain their relative order in the sorted list. It is a comparison-based sorting algorithm and has a time complexity of O(n log n), making it efficient for large datasets.

Another well-known example of a divide and conquer algorithm is the quicksort algorithm. Quicksort is also used for sorting, but it works by selecting a pivot element, partitioning the list into elements less than and greater than the pivot, and then recursively sorting the sublists.

Quicksort has an average-case time complexity of O(n log n) and is often faster in practice than merge sort and other sorting algorithms due to its efficient partitioning.

The divide and conquer strategy is not limited to sorting algorithms. It can be applied to a wide range of problems, including searching, matrix multiplication, and finding the closest pair of points in a two-dimensional plane.

For example, the binary search algorithm is a divide and conquer approach used to search for a specific element in a sorted list. It divides the list in half at each step and compares the target element with the middle element to determine whether it is in the left or right half.

The Karatsuba algorithm is a divide and conquer technique used for fast multiplication of large numbers. It divides the numbers into smaller parts, recursively multiplies them, and then combines the results to obtain the final product.

The closest pair of points problem in computational geometry can also be solved using divide and conquer. It involves dividing the set of points into two subsets, finding the closest pairs in each subset, and then merging the solutions to find the closest pair overall.

In summary, divide and conquer is a powerful problem-solving technique that involves breaking down a complex problem into smaller, more manageable subproblems, solving these subproblems independently, and then combining their solutions to solve the original problem. It is used in various algorithms and has applications in sorting, searching, matrix multiplication, and computational geometry, among others.

Understanding the principles of divide and conquer and its application to specific problems is essential for developing efficient algorithms and solving complex computational tasks.

Applications of the divide and conquer technique extend far beyond sorting algorithms and encompass a wide range of problem-solving domains in computer science and mathematics. One prominent application of divide and conquer is in solving optimization problems, where the goal is to find the best solution among a set of possible solutions.

For example, the famous traveling salesman problem (TSP) is an optimization problem that seeks to find the shortest possible route that visits a set of cities and returns to the starting city. The divide and conquer approach to solving the TSP involves dividing the problem into smaller subproblems by selecting a subset of cities to visit in each step.

The algorithm recursively solves these subproblems and combines their solutions to find the optimal route for the entire problem. This divide and conquer strategy significantly reduces the time complexity of solving large instances of the TSP.

Another application of divide and conquer is in computational geometry, particularly in solving problems related to geometric shapes and arrangements. One such problem is finding the convex hull of a set of points, which is the smallest convex polygon that encloses all the points.

The divide and conquer algorithm for finding the convex hull divides the set of points into smaller subsets, computes the convex hull of each subset, and then merges the convex hulls to obtain the final convex hull of the entire set. This approach efficiently solves the convex hull problem in two or three dimensions.

Divide and conquer can also be applied to polynomial multiplication, a fundamental operation in algebra and computer science. The well-known Karatsuba algorithm, an efficient divide and conquer method, multiplies two polynomials by recursively breaking them into smaller sub-polynomials and then combining the results using a clever technique.

Karatsuba's algorithm reduces the number of required multiplications and improves the overall efficiency of polynomial multiplication, making it a valuable tool in fields like cryptography and computer algebra systems.

In the realm of data science and machine learning, divide and conquer strategies are used for parallel processing and distributed computing. Large datasets can be divided into smaller subsets that are processed independently by multiple computing units, and their results can be combined to obtain the final outcome.

This approach allows for efficient processing of vast amounts of data and is a crucial component of many data analysis and machine learning algorithms.

Parallel sorting algorithms, such as parallel merge sort and parallel quicksort, are examples of divide and conquer techniques adapted for distributed computing environments. These algorithms divide the input data into smaller segments that are sorted in parallel, and then merge the sorted segments to produce the final sorted result.

Divide and conquer also plays a significant role in computer graphics and rendering. One application is in ray tracing, a technique used to simulate the behavior of light in virtual environments.

In ray tracing, the divide and conquer approach is employed to trace rays of light as they interact with surfaces and objects in a scene. By dividing the scene into smaller regions, the algorithm can efficiently compute the paths of individual rays and their interactions with the environment.

Additionally, divide and conquer algorithms are employed in various computational biology and bioinformatics tasks. One such task is sequence alignment, which involves comparing and aligning two or more biological sequences, such as DNA or protein sequences.

Divide and conquer algorithms for sequence alignment break down the problem into smaller sub-alignments and then merge them to obtain the overall alignment. This technique is essential for identifying similarities and differences between biological sequences, aiding in tasks like genome mapping and protein structure prediction.

Furthermore, in the field of numerical analysis, divide and conquer methods are used to solve differential equations and numerical integration problems. These algorithms divide the domain of the problem into smaller intervals, solve the equations or integrals independently in each interval, and then combine the results to approximate the solution.

In scientific computing, divide and conquer techniques enable the efficient simulation of physical phenomena, making them valuable tools for modeling and analysis.

To summarize, the applications of the divide and conquer technique are diverse and extend across various domains within computer science and mathematics. From solving optimization problems like the traveling salesman problem to addressing challenges in computational geometry, polynomial multiplication, and data science, divide and conquer algorithms provide powerful tools for efficient problem-solving.

They are also instrumental in parallel processing, computer graphics, bioinformatics, numerical analysis, and scientific computing, demonstrating their versatility and significance in contemporary research and technology.

Chapter 8: Advanced Data Structures and Their Applications

Specialized data structures are a crucial component of computer science and software development, as they enable the efficient organization and manipulation of data in various problem domains. These data structures are designed to address specific requirements and constraints, optimizing operations such as insertion, retrieval, and deletion for specific use cases.

One well-known specialized data structure is the stack, which follows the Last-In-First-Out (LIFO) principle. Stacks are used for managing data in a way that the most recently added item is the first to be removed. They are employed in parsing expressions, evaluating arithmetic expressions, and tracking function calls in recursion.

Another commonly used specialized data structure is the queue, which adheres to the First-In-First-Out (FIFO) principle. Queues are used when items should be processed in the order they were added. They find applications in tasks such as managing print jobs in an operating system or simulating waiting lines in real-world scenarios.

Priority queues are specialized data structures that extend the basic queue concept by assigning a priority value to each element. Elements with higher priority are processed before those with lower priority. Priority queues are essential for various algorithms, such as Dijkstra's algorithm for finding the shortest path and Huffman coding for data compression.

Heaps, a type of priority queue, are specialized data structures that ensure the highest or lowest priority element is always at the root. Heaps are used in heap sort, a comparison-based sorting algorithm with a time complexity of O(n log n).

Linked lists are another specialized data structure used to store a sequence of elements. Unlike arrays, linked lists do not require contiguous memory and can efficiently insert or delete elements at any position. They are often used for implementing other data structures, like stacks and queues.

Trees are specialized data structures with hierarchical structures that consist of nodes connected by edges. Common types of trees include binary trees, binary search trees (BSTs), and balanced trees like AVL trees and Red-Black trees. BSTs, for instance, are used for efficient searching and sorting operations.

Graphs are versatile specialized data structures consisting of nodes and edges. They find applications in modeling various relationships, such as social networks, transportation systems, and computer networks. Graph algorithms, like breadth-first search (BFS) and depth-first search (DFS), are fundamental tools for exploring and analyzing graphs.

Hash tables, also known as hash maps, are specialized data structures that enable efficient key-value pair storage and retrieval. They are widely used in data indexing, caching, and database management systems. Hash functions play a crucial role in distributing keys evenly across the underlying array to achieve fast access times.

Trie, short for retrieval tree, is a specialized data structure used for efficient string retrieval and storage. Tries are particularly useful for tasks like spell checking, autocomplete, and storing dictionaries. They organize data in a tree-like structure where each node represents a character, and paths from the root to a leaf node form words.

Bloom filters are specialized data structures designed for efficient membership testing. They provide a probabilistic way to check if an element is in a set, often used in database systems and network routing to reduce unnecessary lookups.

Segment trees and Fenwick trees (also known as binary indexed trees) are specialized data structures used for various range query and update operations. They are particularly useful in scenarios where you need to find the minimum, maximum, or sum of elements in a specified range.

Suffix trees and suffix arrays are specialized data structures used for efficient string matching and pattern search in large texts. They are crucial in applications like text indexing, plagiarism detection, and bioinformatics.

Specialized data structures can significantly impact the efficiency and performance of algorithms and applications. Choosing the right data structure for a specific task is a critical decision that can lead to optimized solutions and improved resource utilization.

Understanding the strengths and weaknesses of different data structures, along with their use cases, is essential for software developers and computer scientists alike.

In summary, specialized data structures are fundamental components of computer science and software development. They are designed to address specific requirements and constraints, optimizing data manipulation operations for various problem domains.

From stacks and queues to priority queues, linked lists, trees, graphs, hash tables, tries, Bloom filters, and more, each specialized data structure serves a unique purpose and finds applications in diverse fields.

Choosing the appropriate data structure for a given problem is a crucial aspect of algorithm design and software development, as it can significantly impact the efficiency and performance of solutions.

Advanced data structures, with their specialized designs and efficient operations, find numerous real-world applications in computer science and various industries. One such application is in databases, where B-trees and variations like B+ trees are employed to index and manage large datasets efficiently.

B-trees provide balanced storage and fast retrieval of data, making them ideal for applications that require high-performance database operations, such as indexing records in relational databases and file systems.

Another real-world application of advanced data structures is in geographic information systems (GIS), where spatial data structures like quad-trees and octrees are used to represent and query geographical information. These structures enable efficient storage and retrieval of spatial data, allowing users to find nearby points of interest, perform map overlays, and analyze geographical patterns.

In computer graphics and video games, spatial partitioning data structures like the quadtree and its three-dimensional counterpart, the octree, are essential for efficient collision detection, rendering, and visibility culling. By organizing the scene into hierarchical structures, these data structures enable rapid spatial queries and reduce computational overhead.

In network routing and optimization, advanced data structures like Fibonacci heaps are employed to find the shortest path in weighted graphs efficiently. Fibonacci heaps offer better amortized time complexities compared to traditional data structures, making them valuable in routing protocols and network design.

Machine learning and data mining rely on various advanced data structures for tasks like clustering, nearest neighbor search, and anomaly detection. KD-trees and ball trees, for example, are used to efficiently locate nearest neighbors in multi-dimensional feature spaces, which is crucial for recommendation systems and pattern recognition.

In bioinformatics, suffix trees and suffix arrays play a pivotal role in DNA sequence analysis and string matching. These advanced data structures enable researchers to identify patterns and discover similarities in genetic sequences, aiding in tasks like gene prediction and sequence alignment.

Sparse data structures like compressed sparse row (CSR) and compressed sparse column (CSC) are vital in numerical simulations and scientific computing. They optimize memory usage and matrix-vector operations in solving large linear systems of equations, which is essential in fields like physics, engineering, and computational chemistry.

In data compression, Huffman trees are used to create variable-length codes that efficiently represent data, reducing storage requirements and transmission times. They are widely used in file compression formats like ZIP and image compression standards like JPEG.

Advanced data structures also find applications in natural language processing (NLP), where trie structures are used for efficient dictionary and autocomplete functionalities. Tries allow for fast word lookup and are crucial components of search engines, spelling correction algorithms, and language models.

In financial modeling and risk analysis, Monte Carlo simulations leverage data structures like priority queues and heaps to efficiently sample and analyze a wide range of possible outcomes. These simulations aid in decision-making and risk assessment in the finance industry.

Specialized data structures like bloom filters are used in network security and distributed systems to quickly determine the existence of data in large datasets without revealing the actual data. They are employed in applications such as data deduplication, spam filtering, and distributed caching.

Advanced data structures also have applications in robotics and autonomous navigation. OctoMap, for instance, uses an octree data structure to represent and manage 3D maps of the environment, allowing robots to plan paths and avoid obstacles in real-time.

Furthermore, in recommendation systems and online advertising, collaborative filtering techniques often utilize matrix factorization data structures to analyze user behavior and provide personalized recommendations and advertisements.

In summary, advanced data structures are not abstract concepts confined to the realm of computer science textbooks; they play a vital role in a wide range of real-world applications across diverse industries. From optimizing database operations and GIS analysis to enhancing network routing and supporting machine learning, these data structures empower efficient and effective solutions to complex problems.

Their impact extends to fields as varied as bioinformatics, numerical simulations, data compression, natural language processing, finance, network security, robotics, and recommendation systems.

Understanding and harnessing the potential of advanced data structures are essential skills for researchers, engineers, and developers working in these domains, as they enable the creation of faster, more efficient, and innovative solutions to real-world challenges.

Chapter 9: Advanced Topics in Algorithm Design

Complex algorithmic challenges present intriguing and often formidable problems that require innovative solutions. These challenges can arise in various domains, including computer science, mathematics, engineering, and beyond.

One such challenge is the Traveling Salesman Problem (TSP), which asks for the shortest possible route that visits a set of cities and returns to the starting city. Despite its seemingly simple description, the TSP is an NP-hard problem, meaning that solving it optimally for large datasets becomes computationally infeasible.

The TSP has applications in logistics, manufacturing, and circuit design, where finding an optimal tour can lead to significant cost savings and efficiency improvements.

Another complex problem is the knapsack problem, which involves selecting a subset of items with given weights and values to maximize the total value without exceeding a specified weight limit. The knapsack problem is used in resource allocation, financial portfolio optimization, and even in cutting stock problems, where the goal is to minimize material waste.

Graph coloring, a problem of assigning colors to the vertices of a graph in a way that no adjacent vertices have the same color, is another challenging problem with practical applications. It is used in scheduling tasks, register allocation in compilers, and frequency assignment in wireless communication.

The efficient allocation of resources in network design is a complex challenge that arises in various contexts. For example, the network flow problem involves finding the optimal way to send flow through a network with capacity constraints while maximizing the flow value. This problem has applications in transportation, telecommunications, and supply chain management.

Optimization problems involving linear programming, such as the simplex method, are commonly encountered in operations research and mathematical modeling. They are used for optimizing resource allocation, production planning, and resource management in various industries.

In cryptography, the problem of integer factorization poses a significant challenge with practical implications. Efficiently factoring large integers is crucial for security protocols like RSA encryption, and it remains a complex problem that relies on the factorization of large semiprime numbers.

The traveling salesman problem with time windows (TSPTW) introduces additional constraints by specifying time windows in which cities must be visited. Solving the TSPTW is important in logistics, delivery routing, and vehicle scheduling, where time constraints are critical.

The NP-hard problem of the knapsack with multiple constraints extends the classic knapsack problem by adding multiple constraints on item selection. It is used in resource allocation problems with multiple constraints, such as production planning and resource management in manufacturing.

In computational biology, sequence alignment algorithms tackle complex challenges related to DNA and protein sequence analysis. Dynamic programming algorithms like the Smith-Waterman algorithm are used to find the optimal alignment between sequences, aiding in tasks like gene prediction and sequence homology search.

Graph algorithms like the maximum flow and minimum cut problem are essential in network design and transportation planning. They help optimize the flow of resources in networks with capacity constraints and are used in applications like traffic management and network routing.

Advanced data structures like suffix trees and suffix arrays are employed to efficiently search and analyze large text corpora in natural language processing and information retrieval. They are crucial for tasks like text indexing, plagiarism detection, and search engine optimization.

In computer graphics and image processing, complex challenges arise in rendering realistic scenes and processing images and videos. Ray tracing algorithms, for example, simulate the behavior of light as it interacts with objects in a 3D environment, demanding complex computations for photorealistic rendering.

Numerical simulations in fields like fluid dynamics, climate modeling, and structural engineering involve solving complex partial differential equations. These simulations require high-performance algorithms and supercomputing resources to accurately model real-world phenomena.

Challenges in machine learning and artificial intelligence include training deep neural networks, optimizing hyperparameters, and developing algorithms for reinforcement learning. These challenges have applications in autonomous vehicles, natural language understanding, and recommendation systems.

In quantum computing, complex challenges involve developing quantum algorithms and quantum error correction codes. Quantum algorithms aim to harness the unique properties of quantum bits (qubits) to solve problems faster than classical computers, while error correction is crucial for maintaining the reliability of quantum computations.

The challenge of optimizing code and improving software performance is a constant concern in software development. Profiling, debugging, and optimizing algorithms and data structures are essential tasks for ensuring efficient software operation.

Challenges in data analysis and big data processing include handling massive datasets, performing real-time analytics, and extracting valuable insights. Data scientists and analysts develop algorithms and techniques for processing, visualizing, and interpreting data from diverse sources.

In the emerging field of quantum computing, researchers are tackling complex problems related to quantum algorithms, quantum error correction, and quantum hardware development. Quantum computing has the potential to revolutionize fields like cryptography, optimization, and materials science.

The challenge of developing secure cryptographic algorithms to protect sensitive information is an ongoing concern. Cryptography researchers strive to stay ahead of potential threats by creating robust encryption and decryption methods.

In the realm of cybersecurity, complex challenges include identifying and mitigating vulnerabilities in software and systems, as well as defending against cyberattacks. Security experts use algorithms and techniques to detect, prevent, and respond to security breaches.

Complex algorithmic challenges are pervasive across various domains, and they drive innovation and progress in science, technology, and industry. Solving these challenges requires a deep understanding of algorithms, data structures, mathematical modeling, and computational techniques.

Researchers and practitioners continue to push the boundaries of what is possible, developing new algorithms and methodologies to tackle increasingly complex problems. These challenges fuel advancements in computer science and have far-reaching implications for society, from improving healthcare and transportation to enhancing communication and entertainment.

In summary, complex algorithmic challenges are at the heart of many scientific and technological endeavors. They inspire creativity, drive innovation, and lead to breakthroughs that shape the way we understand and interact with the world.

Problem-solving at an advanced level is a skill that combines creativity, analytical thinking, and deep domain knowledge. It involves tackling complex and multifaceted problems that may not have straightforward solutions.

To excel at advanced problem-solving, one must start by understanding the problem thoroughly. This means breaking it down into its fundamental components, identifying constraints, and defining clear objectives.

The next step is to gather relevant information and data that can inform the problem-solving process. This may involve research, data analysis, or experimentation, depending on the nature of the problem.

Once you have a solid grasp of the problem and the data at hand, it's time to generate potential solutions. Advanced problem solvers often employ techniques like brainstorming, lateral thinking, and concept mapping to explore different approaches.

It's essential to consider both traditional and innovative solutions during this phase. Sometimes, unconventional ideas can lead to breakthrough solutions.

After generating a list of potential solutions, it's crucial to evaluate them rigorously. Consider factors like feasibility, cost-effectiveness, and potential risks.

Advanced problem solvers are not afraid to challenge their assumptions and revisit their problem-solving approach if necessary. Flexibility and adaptability are key traits in this process.

Once a solution is selected, it's time to implement it. This may involve creating a detailed plan, allocating resources, and coordinating efforts with a team.

Effective communication is vital throughout the implementation phase to ensure that everyone involved understands their roles and responsibilities.

During implementation, advanced problem solvers also continuously monitor progress and make adjustments as needed. They are proactive in identifying and addressing any issues that may arise.

Sometimes, a problem-solving process may lead to unexpected challenges or require a change in direction. Being open to adaptation is essential in such cases.

As the implementation phase progresses, advanced problem solvers keep a close eye on the desired outcomes. They use metrics and key performance indicators to measure progress and success.

Advanced problem solvers are also skilled at managing ambiguity and uncertainty. Not all problems have clear-cut solutions, and navigating uncertainty is part of the process.

In some cases, a problem may require ongoing monitoring and adjustment even after the initial solution is implemented. This is especially true for complex, dynamic problems.

One of the most important aspects of advanced problem-solving is the ability to learn from each problem-solving experience. Reflecting on what worked, what didn't, and what could be improved is crucial for personal and professional growth.

Over time, advanced problem solvers develop a toolbox of strategies, techniques, and heuristics that they can apply to different types of problems. They become more efficient and effective problem solvers with each new challenge they face.

Advanced problem-solving skills are highly valued in various fields and industries. They are particularly important in research, engineering, innovation, and leadership roles.

In research, advanced problem solvers are often at the forefront of discoveries and breakthroughs. They have the ability to formulate and test hypotheses, design experiments, and analyze complex data.

In engineering, advanced problem solvers design and optimize systems, products, and processes. They are skilled at identifying and resolving technical challenges.

Innovation relies heavily on advanced problem-solving skills. Innovation often involves pushing the boundaries of what is currently known and finding creative solutions to unmet needs.

Leadership positions, whether in business, academia, or government, require advanced problem-solving abilities. Leaders must make critical decisions, solve complex problems, and navigate uncertainties.

Advanced problem solvers are also valuable in entrepreneurship and startup environments. Starting and scaling a business often involves solving a series of complex challenges.

The ability to solve problems at an advanced level is not limited to specific fields or professions. It is a transferable skill that can benefit individuals in various aspects of their lives.

In personal life, advanced problem solvers are often more resourceful and resilient in the face of adversity. They have the confidence to tackle difficult situations and find solutions.

Education plays a crucial role in developing advanced problem-solving skills. Courses in critical thinking, decision making, and problem solving can help individuals hone their abilities.

Additionally, exposure to diverse experiences and perspectives can broaden one's problem-solving toolkit. Interacting with people from different backgrounds and cultures can offer fresh insights and approaches to problem solving.

Mentorship and collaboration are also valuable for developing advanced problem-solving skills. Working with experienced mentors and collaborating with peers on challenging projects can provide valuable learning opportunities.

In summary, problem-solving at an advanced level is a multifaceted skill that combines creativity, analytical thinking, and domain knowledge. It involves understanding complex problems, generating innovative solutions, evaluating them rigorously, and implementing them effectively.

Advanced problem solvers are flexible, adaptable, and open to learning from each problem-solving experience. They are highly valued in various fields and industries and can benefit from education, diverse experiences, mentorship, and collaboration.

Ultimately, advanced problem-solving skills are transferable and valuable in both personal and professional contexts.

Chapter 10: Mastering Algorithms: Expert-level Techniques and Challenges

Expert algorithmic techniques represent the pinnacle of problem-solving proficiency, encompassing advanced strategies and methodologies. These techniques are employed by seasoned computer scientists, mathematicians, and engineers to tackle the most challenging computational problems.

One key aspect of expert algorithmic techniques is the ability to formulate problems precisely and mathematically. This involves translating real-world scenarios and challenges into well-defined mathematical models, which can then be analyzed and solved algorithmically.

Advanced algorithmic practitioners often employ mathematical proofs to validate the correctness and efficiency of their algorithms. Proofs provide rigorous guarantees that a given algorithm will produce the desired results within specified constraints.

Expert algorithmic techniques frequently leverage the power of abstraction and problem decomposition. By breaking down complex problems into smaller, more manageable subproblems, algorithm designers can develop elegant and efficient solutions.

Sophisticated data structures are at the core of many expert algorithmic techniques. These data structures are carefully chosen and designed to optimize specific operations, such as insertion, retrieval, and traversal.

In-depth knowledge of computational complexity theory is essential for advanced algorithm designers. This understanding enables them to classify problems into complexity classes and determine the inherent difficulty of solving them.

Expert algorithmic practitioners are adept at analyzing the time and space complexity of their algorithms. They can predict how an algorithm's performance will scale with increasing problem sizes and data inputs.

Advanced algorithmic techniques often draw inspiration from various mathematical fields, including graph theory, number theory, linear algebra, and combinatorics. By applying mathematical concepts creatively, algorithm designers can develop novel solutions to complex problems.

Dynamic programming is a powerful technique employed by experts to solve problems by breaking them down into overlapping subproblems and caching intermediate results. This approach can dramatically reduce redundant calculations and improve computational efficiency.

Greedy algorithms are another strategy used by advanced practitioners to make locally optimal choices at each step, aiming for a globally optimal solution. Greedy algorithms are particularly useful for optimization problems with well-defined criteria.

Expert algorithm designers are skilled in the art of algorithmic problem reduction. They can transform one problem into another with similar characteristics, potentially simplifying the solution process.

Efficient heuristic algorithms are frequently employed to find approximate solutions to computationally intractable problems. Heuristics provide practical and often satisfactory results when finding the exact solution is too time-consuming.

Metaheuristic algorithms, such as genetic algorithms, simulated annealing, and particle swarm optimization, are powerful tools for exploring solution spaces and finding near-optimal solutions.

In advanced algorithmic techniques, the use of probabilistic algorithms is common, particularly in situations where a probabilistic approach can yield results quickly with a high probability of correctness.

Experts in algorithm design often employ parallel and distributed computing techniques to harness the power of multiple processors or computers, enabling the efficient solution of large-scale problems.

Advanced algorithmic practitioners are skilled in algorithmic design patterns. These patterns are reusable templates for solving common types of problems and are valuable for streamlining the development process.

Expertise in algorithmic optimization is a hallmark of advanced algorithm designers. They can fine-tune algorithms and data structures to squeeze out every bit of performance.

Experts often engage in algorithmic competitions and challenges to hone their skills and learn from their peers. Competitions like the ACM International Collegiate Programming Contest (ICPC) and online platforms like Codeforces and LeetCode provide opportunities for algorithmic enthusiasts to test their mettle.

Proficiency in algorithm visualization is another skill that distinguishes advanced practitioners. Visualizing algorithms helps in understanding their behavior, identifying bottlenecks, and improving overall design.

Advanced algorithmic techniques extend beyond the realm of computer science and have applications in various domains. In computational biology, experts use sophisticated algorithms to analyze DNA sequences, predict protein structures, and discover patterns in biological data.

In finance, advanced algorithms are employed for high-frequency trading, risk management, portfolio optimization, and option pricing.

Transportation and logistics benefit from expert algorithmic techniques to optimize routes, minimize costs, and efficiently allocate resources.

In artificial intelligence and machine learning, advanced algorithms are instrumental in training complex deep neural networks, optimizing hyperparameters, and developing reinforcement learning agents.

The gaming industry relies on advanced algorithms for creating realistic simulations, generating procedural content, and implementing intelligent non-player characters (NPCs).

In natural language processing (NLP), experts use advanced algorithms for machine translation, sentiment analysis, and text summarization.

Experts in algorithm design play a crucial role in developing cryptographic algorithms to secure communication and protect sensitive information.

In healthcare, advanced algorithms are used for medical image analysis, drug discovery, and patient diagnosis.

Astronomers and astrophysicists employ advanced algorithms to process vast amounts of astronomical data, detect celestial objects, and model complex astrophysical phenomena.

Environmental scientists use advanced algorithms to model climate change, predict natural disasters, and analyze environmental data.

Advanced algorithmic techniques have even found applications in the arts, with algorithms generating intricate visual patterns, composing music, and creating interactive artworks.

In summary, expert algorithmic techniques represent the pinnacle of problem-solving proficiency. Advanced algorithm designers possess a deep understanding of mathematical modeling, data structures, computational complexity, and algorithm analysis.

They employ a wide range of strategies, from dynamic programming and greedy algorithms to heuristic and metaheuristic techniques, to tackle complex problems efficiently.

Expert algorithmic techniques have far-reaching applications across numerous domains, from computer science and finance to healthcare, astronomy, and the arts.

The ability to apply advanced algorithmic techniques is a testament to the creativity and ingenuity of those who dedicate themselves to the craft of algorithm design.

Tackling advanced algorithmic challenges requires a deep and multifaceted understanding of algorithms, data structures, and problem-solving techniques. It is a journey that demands creativity, analytical thinking, and perseverance.

Advanced algorithmic challenges often involve problems that are computationally intractable, meaning that finding exact solutions in a reasonable amount of time is highly unlikely.

One approach to tackling such challenges is approximation algorithms, which aim to find near-optimal solutions within a feasible time frame. These algorithms sacrifice optimality for efficiency and are valuable in situations where exact solutions are elusive.

Another strategy is to explore heuristic algorithms, which provide practical solutions by making educated guesses and trade-offs. Heuristics are effective when finding the best solution is prohibitively expensive in terms of time and resources.

In the realm of advanced algorithmic challenges, randomized algorithms play a significant role. These algorithms introduce an element of randomness in their decision-making process, which can lead to faster solutions with high confidence levels.

Tackling advanced algorithmic challenges often begins with problem modeling, where the problem statement is translated into a mathematical or computational form. This step is crucial for developing algorithmic solutions.

Mathematical proofs and formal analysis are essential tools for understanding the properties and limitations of the problems and algorithms involved.

Advanced algorithmic practitioners are skilled in conducting worst-case and average-case analyses to assess the performance of their algorithms under different scenarios.

Dynamic programming is a technique frequently employed to solve complex problems by breaking them down into overlapping subproblems. This approach reduces redundant calculations and improves algorithmic efficiency.

Divide and conquer strategies, which involve recursively breaking a problem into smaller subproblems, are another powerful tool for tackling advanced algorithmic challenges.

Expert algorithm designers are adept at recognizing similarities between different problems and reusing or adapting existing algorithmic solutions.

Parallel and distributed computing techniques are often leveraged to tackle advanced algorithmic challenges. These techniques harness the computational power of multiple processors or computers to solve large-scale problems efficiently.

Algorithmic optimization is a crucial aspect of addressing advanced challenges. Experts fine-tune algorithms and data structures to achieve optimal performance and scalability.

In some cases, advanced algorithmic challenges require the development of custom data structures tailored to the problem's characteristics.

Advanced algorithmic practitioners are skilled in navigating the trade-offs between time complexity and space complexity, optimizing their algorithms for specific resource constraints.

Advanced algorithmic challenges are not limited to the realm of computer science but extend to various domains.

In computational biology, researchers grapple with complex problems such as sequence alignment, phylogenetic tree reconstruction, and protein structure prediction.

In finance, algorithmic challenges involve optimizing trading strategies, risk assessment, and portfolio management in a high-frequency trading environment.

Transportation and logistics rely on advanced algorithms for route optimization, vehicle scheduling, and supply chain management.

Machine learning and artificial intelligence present their own set of challenges, including training deep neural networks, optimizing model parameters, and developing reinforcement learning algorithms.

Natural language processing poses advanced algorithmic challenges in tasks such as machine translation, sentiment analysis, and speech recognition.

Cryptography and cybersecurity demand the development of secure cryptographic algorithms and efficient methods for detecting and mitigating cyber threats.

Healthcare leverages advanced algorithms for medical image analysis, disease diagnosis, drug discovery, and personalized treatment recommendations.

Astronomy and astrophysics involve complex computational challenges in data analysis, celestial object detection, and cosmological simulations.

Environmental scientists use advanced algorithms to model climate change, predict natural disasters, and analyze environmental data.

Complex algorithmic challenges also arise in gaming, where developers aim to create realistic simulations, generate procedural content, and implement intelligent non-player characters (NPCs).

In the arts, algorithms play a role in generating intricate visual patterns, composing music, and creating interactive artworks.

Tackling advanced algorithmic challenges often involves interdisciplinary collaboration, with experts from various fields working together to address complex problems.

The development of quantum algorithms and quantum error correction codes represents a cutting-edge frontier in advanced algorithmic research.

Quantum computing promises to revolutionize many fields by solving problems that are currently beyond the reach of classical computers.

As quantum computing evolves, it opens up new avenues for tackling advanced algorithmic challenges in cryptography, optimization, and scientific simulations.

Addressing advanced algorithmic challenges is not a solitary endeavor. It requires a community of dedicated researchers, practitioners, and enthusiasts who share knowledge, collaborate, and push the boundaries of what is possible.

The pursuit of advanced algorithmic solutions is a journey filled with intellectual curiosity and the excitement of discovery. It is a testament to human ingenuity and the relentless quest to unravel the mysteries of the universe, optimize processes, and improve the human condition.

In summary, tackling advanced algorithmic challenges is a complex and multifaceted endeavor that spans various domains and requires a deep understanding of algorithms, data structures, and problem-solving techniques.

From approximation algorithms and heuristics to randomized algorithms and dynamic programming, a wide range of strategies are employed to find solutions to computationally intractable problems.

Advanced algorithmic practitioners possess the skills to model problems mathematically, conduct formal analyses, and optimize algorithms and data structures for efficiency.

These challenges extend beyond computer science, impacting fields such as biology, finance, transportation, machine learning, cryptography, healthcare, and many others.

Interdisciplinary collaboration and the exploration of quantum computing are expanding the frontiers of advanced algorithmic research.

Tackling advanced algorithmic challenges is a collaborative and inspiring journey that drives innovation and pushes the boundaries of human knowledge and capabilities.

BOOK 3
ALGORITHMIC MASTERY
A JOURNEY FROM NOVICE TO GURU

ROB BOTWRIGHT

Chapter 1: Embarking on the Algorithmic Journey

Introduction to computer science is a gateway to understanding the fundamental principles of computing and information technology. It is a field that encompasses a wide range of topics, from the theoretical foundations of computation to the practical aspects of software development and hardware design.

At its core, computer science is concerned with the study of algorithms, which are step-by-step instructions for solving problems. These algorithms can be implemented in various programming languages to perform tasks and manipulate data.

The history of computer science is marked by significant milestones, including the development of the first programmable computers in the mid-20th century. These early machines laid the foundation for modern computing and paved the way for the digital revolution.

One of the key figures in the history of computer science is Alan Turing, whose concept of the Turing machine introduced the idea of a universal computing device capable of executing any algorithm.

Theoretical computer science explores the mathematical underpinnings of computation, including formal languages, automata theory, and complexity theory. These areas help computer scientists analyze the limitations and capabilities of algorithms and machines.

The practical application of computer science extends to various fields, including artificial intelligence, data science, cybersecurity, and software engineering.

Artificial intelligence focuses on creating computer systems that can simulate human intelligence, enabling tasks like natural language processing, image recognition, and decision making.

Data science involves extracting knowledge and insights from large datasets through techniques such as data mining, machine learning, and statistical analysis.

Cybersecurity is crucial for protecting computer systems and networks from unauthorized access, data breaches, and cyberattacks.

Software engineering is the discipline of designing, developing, and maintaining software systems, ensuring they meet functional requirements and are reliable and maintainable.

Computer scientists use a wide range of tools and technologies, including programming languages, software development frameworks, and hardware components, to build innovative solutions.

The field of computer science has a strong connection to mathematics, as mathematical concepts and methods are often used to analyze and design algorithms.

Computer scientists also draw from fields like physics, electrical engineering, and cognitive science to gain insights into how computers work and how humans interact with them.

In recent years, the rapid advancement of technology has led to the emergence of new areas within computer science, such as quantum computing, blockchain technology, and the Internet of Things (IoT).

Quantum computing leverages the principles of quantum mechanics to perform computations that are infeasible for classical computers, potentially revolutionizing fields like cryptography and optimization.

Blockchain technology, known for its use in cryptocurrencies like Bitcoin, is a decentralized ledger system that has applications in secure data sharing and digital contracts.

The Internet of Things (IoT) connects everyday objects to the internet, enabling them to collect and exchange data, leading to innovations in smart homes, healthcare, and transportation.

Computer science is a dynamic field that continues to evolve rapidly, driven by ongoing technological advancements and the demand for innovative solutions.

To excel in computer science, individuals must develop problem-solving skills, logical reasoning, and a deep understanding of algorithms and data structures.

Programming is a fundamental skill in computer science, as it allows individuals to translate their ideas into working software applications.

Popular programming languages include Python, Java, C++, and JavaScript, each with its own strengths and applications.

Computer scientists often work collaboratively in teams to develop software systems and tackle complex problems.

Communication skills are essential, as computer scientists must be able to explain their ideas, collaborate with colleagues, and convey technical information to non-technical stakeholders.

Ethical considerations are also important in computer science, as professionals are responsible for ensuring the privacy, security, and ethical use of technology.

The impact of computer science on society is profound, influencing virtually every aspect of modern life.

In healthcare, computer science contributes to medical imaging, drug discovery, and patient record management.

In transportation, computer algorithms are used for traffic management, route optimization, and autonomous vehicle control.

In finance, computer-based trading systems execute high-speed transactions, and data analytics inform investment decisions.

In education, computer science is increasingly recognized as a fundamental skill, with coding and computational thinking incorporated into curricula.

The advent of the internet has transformed communication, commerce, and entertainment, connecting people and information globally.

As computer science continues to advance, it presents both opportunities and challenges.

Ethical concerns related to privacy, security, and artificial intelligence ethics are areas of ongoing research and discussion.

The future of computer science holds exciting possibilities, from breakthroughs in quantum computing to innovations in human-computer interaction and artificial intelligence.

In summary, introduction to computer science provides a foundational understanding of the principles, theories, and applications that drive this dynamic field.

It encompasses a wide range of topics, from algorithms and data structures to artificial intelligence and cybersecurity.

Computer scientists play a pivotal role in shaping the technology-driven world, developing solutions that impact society, business, and individuals.

To embark on a journey in computer science is to explore a realm of infinite possibilities, where creativity, logic, and innovation converge to shape the future of technology and human progress.

The role of algorithms in problem solving is fundamental to computer science and beyond. Algorithms are step-by-step procedures or sets of instructions for solving specific problems or performing tasks efficiently.

They serve as a blueprint for solving problems in a systematic and repeatable manner. In computer science, algorithms are the driving force behind software development, enabling the creation of applications that range from simple calculators to complex artificial intelligence systems.

Algorithms are the foundation of modern technology, underpinning everything from search engines and social media platforms to autonomous vehicles and medical diagnostics.

One of the key characteristics of algorithms is that they are agnostic to the programming language or technology used for implementation. This means that the same algorithm can be implemented in different languages or on different hardware platforms, allowing for flexibility and versatility.

The study of algorithms encompasses a wide range of topics, including algorithm design, analysis, and optimization. Algorithm design involves the creative process of developing efficient solutions to real-world problems.

Analyzing algorithms is essential to understand their performance characteristics, such as time complexity and space complexity. These analyses help computer scientists determine how algorithms will perform under different conditions and for various input sizes.

Optimizing algorithms involves making improvements to reduce their resource consumption, such as minimizing execution time or memory usage. Efficient algorithms can have a significant impact on the speed and scalability of software applications.

The importance of algorithms in problem solving extends beyond the field of computer science. Algorithms are used in various domains, including mathematics, engineering, economics, and natural sciences.

In mathematics, algorithms play a crucial role in solving mathematical problems, such as finding prime numbers, calculating derivatives, and solving equations.

In engineering, algorithms are used for tasks like circuit design, optimization of mechanical systems, and signal processing.

Economists use algorithms for economic modeling, forecasting, and optimization of resource allocation.

Natural scientists rely on algorithms to analyze experimental data, simulate physical processes, and model complex natural phenomena.

One of the fundamental challenges in algorithm design is finding the most efficient solution to a problem. Efficiency is typically measured in terms of time complexity and space complexity.

Time complexity quantifies the amount of time an algorithm takes to complete its task as a function of the input size. Common time complexity classes include constant time ($O(1)$), logarithmic time ($O(\log n)$), linear time ($O(n)$), and exponential time ($O(2^n)$).

Space complexity measures the amount of memory or storage space required by an algorithm as a function of the input size. Space complexity classes include constant space ($O(1)$), linear space ($O(n)$), and quadratic space ($O(n^2)$).

Algorithm designers strive to develop algorithms with low time and space complexity to ensure efficient performance. Achieving optimal complexity often involves trade-offs and creative problem-solving.

Dynamic programming is a technique frequently used to optimize algorithms by storing and reusing intermediate results. This approach is especially useful for problems with overlapping subproblems, such as the Fibonacci sequence or the shortest path in a graph.

Greedy algorithms are another strategy employed to solve optimization problems by making locally optimal choices at each step. While not always guaranteeing the global optimum, greedy algorithms can provide efficient solutions for specific problem types.

Divide and conquer is a problem-solving paradigm where a complex problem is broken down into smaller subproblems that are easier to solve. These subproblems are then solved recursively, and their solutions are combined to solve the original problem.

Efficient sorting algorithms are essential tools in computer science and data processing. Algorithms like quicksort, mergesort, and heapsort allow for efficient arrangement of data in ascending or descending order.

Searching algorithms are used to find specific items or values within a dataset. Binary search is a well-known algorithm for searching in sorted arrays, offering a time complexity of $O(\log n)$.

Graph algorithms are essential for solving problems related to networks, social graphs, and route optimization. Algorithms for graph traversal, shortest path calculation, and minimum spanning trees are widely used in various applications.

Dynamic programming is a powerful technique employed to solve problems by breaking them down into overlapping subproblems and caching intermediate results. This approach can dramatically reduce redundant calculations and improve computational efficiency.

Greedy algorithms are another strategy used by algorithm designers to make locally optimal choices at each step, aiming for a globally optimal solution. Greedy algorithms are particularly useful for optimization problems with well-defined criteria.

Expert algorithmic practitioners are skilled in the art of algorithmic problem reduction. They can transform one problem into another with similar characteristics, potentially simplifying the solution process.

Efficient heuristic algorithms are frequently employed to find approximate solutions to computationally intractable problems. Heuristics provide practical and often satisfactory results when finding the exact solution is too time-consuming.

Metaheuristic algorithms, such as genetic algorithms, simulated annealing, and particle swarm optimization, are powerful tools for exploring solution spaces and finding near-optimal solutions.

In advanced algorithmic techniques, the use of probabilistic algorithms is common, particularly in situations where a probabilistic approach can yield results quickly with a high probability of correctness.

Experts in algorithm design often employ parallel and distributed computing techniques to harness the power of multiple processors or computers, enabling the efficient solution of large-scale problems.

Advanced algorithmic practitioners are skilled in algorithmic design patterns. These patterns are reusable templates for solving common types of problems and are valuable for streamlining the development process.

Expertise in algorithmic optimization is a hallmark of advanced algorithm designers. They can fine-tune algorithms and data structures to squeeze out every bit of performance.

Experts often engage in algorithmic competitions and challenges to hone their skills and learn from their peers. Competitions like the ACM International Collegiate Programming Contest (ICPC) and online platforms like Codeforces and LeetCode provide opportunities for algorithmic enthusiasts to test their mettle.

Proficiency in algorithm visualization is another skill that distinguishes advanced practitioners. Visualizing algorithms helps in understanding their behavior, identifying bottlenecks, and improving overall design.

Advanced algorithmic techniques extend beyond the realm of computer science and have applications in various domains. In computational biology, experts use sophisticated algorithms to analyze DNA sequences, predict protein structures, and discover patterns in biological data.

In finance, advanced algorithms are employed for high-frequency trading, risk management, portfolio optimization, and option pricing.

Transportation and logistics benefit from expert algorithmic techniques to optimize routes, minimize costs, and efficiently allocate resources.

In artificial intelligence and machine learning, advanced algorithms are instrumental in training complex deep neural networks, optimizing hyperparameters, and developing reinforcement learning agents.

The gaming industry relies on advanced algorithms for creating realistic simulations, generating procedural content, and implementing intelligent non-player characters (NPCs).

In natural language processing (NLP), experts use advanced algorithms for machine translation, sentiment analysis, and text summarization.

Experts in algorithm design play a crucial role in developing cryptographic algorithms to secure communication and protect sensitive information.

In healthcare, advanced algorithms are used for medical image analysis, drug discovery, and patient diagnosis.

Astronomers and astrophysicists employ advanced algorithms to process vast amounts of astronomical data, detect celestial objects, and model complex astrophysical phenomena.

Environmental scientists use advanced algorithms to model climate change, predict natural disasters, and analyze environmental data.

Advanced algorithmic techniques have even found applications in the arts, with algorithms generating intricate visual patterns, composing music, and creating interactive artworks.

In summary, expert algorithmic techniques represent the pinnacle of problem-solving proficiency. Advanced algorithm designers possess a deep understanding of mathematical modeling, data structures, computational complexity, and algorithm analysis.

They employ a wide range of strategies, from dynamic programming and greedy algorithms to heuristic and metaheuristic techniques, to tackle complex problems efficiently.

Their expertise extends beyond computer science, impacting fields like biology, finance, transportation, artificial intelligence, and many others.

As technology continues to advance, the role of advanced algorithms in shaping the future of problem-solving remains central.

These experts drive innovation, optimize processes, and push the boundaries of what is achievable, making a significant impact on our digital world and society at large.

Chapter 2: The Basics of Algorithmic Thinking

The algorithmic problem-solving process is a systematic approach to addressing complex challenges. It involves breaking down a problem into manageable components, designing algorithms to solve them, implementing those algorithms in code, and evaluating the results.

The first step in this process is problem understanding. To effectively solve a problem, one must thoroughly understand its requirements, constraints, and objectives.

Clear problem understanding lays the foundation for defining the problem's scope and its desired outcomes. Once the problem is well-defined, the next step is to devise a plan for solving it.

Algorithm design is at the heart of the problem-solving process. It entails creating a logical sequence of steps that, when executed, will lead to a solution.

Algorithm design involves careful consideration of data structures, computational complexity, and efficiency. It may require drawing upon various algorithmic techniques, such as dynamic programming, greedy algorithms, or divide and conquer.

During this phase, it's crucial to think critically and creatively, exploring different approaches and strategies for tackling the problem. Once an algorithm is conceptualized, it should be documented and represented in a clear and unambiguous manner.

The documentation typically includes pseudocode, flowcharts, or written descriptions that outline the steps of the algorithm. This documentation serves as a blueprint for the implementation phase.

The next step in the algorithmic problem-solving process is implementation. Here, the designed algorithm is translated into a programming language, transforming the abstract solution into executable code.

The implementation phase requires attention to detail, as even small errors can have significant consequences. Debugging and testing are essential parts of this phase, ensuring that the code functions correctly and efficiently.

Programming languages offer a variety of tools and libraries that can be leveraged to simplify the implementation process. These tools can help with tasks such as data manipulation, user interface design, and input/output operations.

Once the code is complete and thoroughly tested, the algorithm can be applied to real-world data or scenarios. This is the evaluation phase, where the effectiveness and efficiency of the algorithm are assessed.

Evaluating the algorithm involves running it on representative inputs and measuring its performance. Performance metrics may include execution time, memory usage, and the algorithm's ability to produce accurate results.

The results of the evaluation provide valuable feedback on the algorithm's performance and may reveal opportunities for optimization or improvement. If the algorithm meets the desired criteria and solves the problem effectively, it can be considered a success.

However, if the algorithm falls short in any way, it may be necessary to revisit the design and implementation phases to make necessary adjustments. This iterative approach allows for continuous refinement and enhancement of the algorithm.

Throughout the algorithmic problem-solving process, it's essential to maintain a problem-solving mindset. This includes being open to new ideas, considering alternative approaches, and persevering in the face of challenges.

Collaboration and communication are also vital aspects of the process. Sharing ideas, seeking input from peers, and explaining the problem-solving rationale can lead to more robust solutions.

The algorithmic problem-solving process is not limited to a single iteration. In many cases, it involves a cycle of refinement and optimization as new information or requirements emerge.

Furthermore, the process can be applied to a wide range of domains and disciplines. From mathematics and computer science to engineering, biology, and economics, the principles of algorithmic problem solving are universally applicable.

In summary, the algorithmic problem-solving process is a structured approach to addressing complex problems. It begins with problem understanding and definition, followed by algorithm design, implementation, and evaluation.

Throughout the process, creativity, attention to detail, and a willingness to adapt are essential qualities. The outcome of successful algorithmic problem solving is the development of effective solutions that address real-world challenges.

As technology continues to advance and problems become increasingly complex, the ability to apply this problem-solving process becomes ever more valuable.

Whether solving practical engineering problems, optimizing business processes, or unraveling intricate scientific phenomena, the algorithmic problem-solving process serves as a powerful tool for innovation and progress.

Algorithmic design principles form the foundation of effective problem-solving in computer science and related fields. These principles encompass a set of guidelines and best practices for creating algorithms that are efficient, reliable, and maintainable.

One of the fundamental principles of algorithmic design is simplicity. Simple algorithms are easier to understand, debug, and maintain, making them a preferred choice in most cases.

Simplicity encourages the use of straightforward and intuitive solutions that are less prone to errors. Complexity should only be introduced when it is necessary to address the specific requirements of a problem.

Another key principle is modularity, which involves breaking down complex problems into smaller, manageable subproblems. Each subproblem can be solved independently, and the solutions can then be combined to solve the original problem.

Modularity enhances code reusability, as well-designed modules can be used in different contexts or even in future projects. It also simplifies the debugging process, as errors can be isolated to specific modules and addressed more effectively.

Efficiency is a critical consideration in algorithmic design. Efficient algorithms are those that consume minimal computational resources, such as time and memory, to achieve their goals.

Efficiency can often be measured using metrics like time complexity and space complexity, which quantify the algorithm's resource usage. Efficient algorithms are preferred because they can handle larger input sizes, respond quickly, and reduce operational costs.

However, efficiency should be balanced with other considerations, such as simplicity and maintainability. In some cases, achieving the utmost efficiency may lead to overly complex and difficult-to-maintain code.

Scalability is closely related to efficiency and refers to an algorithm's ability to handle larger and more demanding workloads. Scalable algorithms can adapt to increased input sizes or growing data volumes without a significant drop in performance.

Scalability is essential in modern computing environments, where data and processing demands are constantly increasing. Well-designed algorithms can scale horizontally or vertically to meet these demands.

Another important principle is correctness, which emphasizes the need for algorithms to produce accurate and dependable results. Correctness is a non-negotiable requirement, as algorithms that produce incorrect results can have serious consequences.

To ensure correctness, algorithms must be thoroughly tested against a variety of inputs, including edge cases and boundary conditions. Formal methods, such as mathematical proofs, can also be used to establish the correctness of an algorithm.

Robustness is closely related to correctness and refers to an algorithm's ability to handle unexpected or erroneous inputs gracefully. Robust algorithms are designed to detect and handle errors without crashing or producing incorrect results.

Error handling, input validation, and graceful degradation are some techniques used to enhance algorithmic robustness. These practices ensure that the algorithm remains reliable even in challenging or unpredictable situations.

The principle of generality encourages the creation of algorithms that can be applied to a wide range of problems. General algorithms are versatile and adaptable, making them valuable tools in various domains.

General algorithms often employ abstractions and parameterization to make them applicable to different situations. By designing algorithms with generality in mind, developers can reduce the need for specialized, one-off solutions.

An essential aspect of algorithmic design is maintainability. Maintainable algorithms are those that can be easily modified, extended, or adapted to accommodate changing requirements.

Documentation, code comments, and clear naming conventions are essential for ensuring the maintainability of algorithms. Well-documented code allows developers to understand the algorithm's purpose and implementation details, facilitating future modifications.

Another important principle is elegance, which encourages the creation of algorithms that are not only functional but also aesthetically pleasing. Elegant algorithms are often characterized by their simplicity, efficiency, and clarity.

Elegance is a subjective concept, but it reflects the idea that beautiful code is not only easier to understand but also more enjoyable to work with. Elegant algorithms are a testament to the artistry of computer science.

In addition to these principles, algorithmic design often involves trade-offs and compromises. Balancing conflicting objectives, such as efficiency and simplicity, is a common challenge in algorithm development.

The choice of data structures is also a crucial aspect of algorithmic design. Data structures provide a way to organize and store data, and the selection of an appropriate data structure can significantly impact an algorithm's performance.

Common data structures include arrays, linked lists, trees, queues, and hash tables, each with its own strengths and weaknesses. Choosing the right data structure depends on the specific requirements of the algorithm and the problem it aims to solve.

The process of algorithmic design is iterative, involving multiple rounds of refinement and optimization. It often begins with a high-level understanding of the problem and the development of a preliminary algorithm.

As the design process progresses, the algorithm is refined, tested, and evaluated to identify areas for improvement. This iterative approach allows developers to incrementally enhance the algorithm's performance and maintainability.

Algorithmic design is not limited to any particular programming language or technology. It is a fundamental skill that transcends specific tools and can be applied across a wide range of domains and platforms.

Moreover, algorithmic design is a creative endeavor that requires problem-solving skills, critical thinking, and a deep understanding of computational concepts. It is a discipline that combines science and art, where developers strive to create elegant, efficient, and reliable solutions to complex problems.

In summary, algorithmic design principles guide the development of effective algorithms that are both efficient and maintainable. These principles encompass simplicity, modularity, efficiency, scalability, correctness, robustness, generality, and elegance.

Algorithmic design involves trade-offs and compromises and often requires careful consideration of data structures and iterative refinement.

Ultimately, algorithmic design is a creative and versatile skill that empowers developers to tackle complex problems in diverse domains, making it a cornerstone of computer science and software engineering.

Chapter 3: Algorithm Analysis and Efficiency

Time and space complexity analysis is a fundamental aspect of algorithm design and evaluation. It involves quantifying the resources an algorithm requires in terms of time and memory.

Time complexity, in particular, measures the computational time an algorithm needs to solve a problem. It helps us understand how the algorithm's performance scales with input size.

In time complexity analysis, we often express an algorithm's performance as a function of the input size, denoted as "n." Common notations used include O(n), O(n log n), O(n^2), and more, representing different growth rates.

The "O" notation, known as Big O notation, is a widely used tool for describing time complexity. It provides an upper bound on the growth rate of an algorithm's runtime.

For example, an algorithm with a time complexity of O(n) means that its runtime increases linearly with the input size. If you double the input size, the algorithm will take approximately twice as long to execute.

On the other hand, an algorithm with a time complexity of O(n^2) implies that its runtime increases quadratically with input size. In this case, doubling the input size will result in the algorithm taking approximately four times longer to run.

Time complexity analysis helps us compare different algorithms for the same problem and choose the most efficient one.

It also allows us to make informed decisions about algorithm selection when dealing with large datasets or time-critical applications.

However, time complexity analysis is an abstract measure and does not account for hardware-specific details, constant factors, or low-level optimizations.

Space complexity analysis, on the other hand, focuses on quantifying the amount of memory an algorithm consumes. It helps us understand how an algorithm's memory usage scales with input size.

Similar to time complexity analysis, space complexity is expressed in terms of the input size "n."

Space complexity analysis is crucial for optimizing memory usage, especially in resource-constrained environments.

Efficient algorithms aim to minimize both time and space complexity, achieving a balance between computational speed and memory usage.

In practice, optimizing time and space complexity often involves trade-offs. Reducing memory usage may lead to increased computation time, and vice versa.

Analyzing an algorithm's time and space complexity often involves mathematical proofs, counting operations, and considering worst-case scenarios.

Worst-case analysis assumes that the algorithm encounters the input that requires the maximum amount of time or memory.

Average-case analysis, on the other hand, considers the expected performance over all possible inputs, weighted by their probabilities.

Best-case analysis examines the algorithm's performance under ideal conditions, which may not be very informative in most cases.

The choice between these analysis methods depends on the problem and the information needed to make informed decisions.

Time and space complexity analysis also helps in identifying bottlenecks in algorithms. By understanding where an algorithm spends most of its time or memory, developers can target specific areas for optimization.

Profiling tools and performance analysis techniques complement theoretical complexity analysis by providing real-world insights into an algorithm's behavior.

In addition to analyzing individual algorithms, complexity analysis plays a crucial role in the design and analysis of data structures.

Efficient data structures can significantly impact the time and space complexity of algorithms that use them.

For example, a well-designed hash table can offer constant-time average-case access, reducing the time complexity of operations.

Similarly, efficient data structures like balanced trees can optimize search and insertion operations, improving overall algorithm performance.

It's important to note that time and space complexity analysis provides an abstract view of algorithmic performance. Real-world scenarios may involve additional factors, such as input distribution, hardware architecture, and system load.

Empirical testing and benchmarking are essential for validating the theoretical predictions of complexity analysis.

In practice, many factors can influence an algorithm's performance, including input data characteristics and the specific hardware and software environment.

Professionals and researchers use complexity analysis as a starting point for algorithm development and optimization.

It guides the selection of appropriate algorithms and data structures for specific tasks, ensuring efficient use of computational resources.

Complexity analysis also aids in understanding the limits of computation. For problems with high time or space complexity, it may be necessary to explore alternative algorithmic approaches or leverage parallel computing.

As technology evolves, the importance of time and space complexity analysis remains paramount. Efficient algorithms are at the core of many applications, from web search engines and data processing to scientific simulations and artificial intelligence.

In summary, time and space complexity analysis are essential tools for algorithm design and evaluation. They provide a framework for quantifying an algorithm's resource requirements in terms of time and memory.

Complexity analysis helps us make informed decisions about algorithm selection, optimization, and data structure design.

While it offers valuable insights, complexity analysis is a theoretical model and should be complemented by empirical testing and profiling in real-world scenarios.

Efficient algorithms and data structures are the foundation of modern computing, driving innovation and enabling the development of complex systems and applications.

Big O notation is a mathematical notation used in computer science and mathematics to describe the upper bound on the growth rate of a function. It provides a way to express how the runtime or space requirements of an algorithm scale as the input size increases.

The "O" in Big O stands for "order of" or "order," and it is followed by a mathematical function or expression. For example, O(n) represents linear time complexity, indicating that an algorithm's runtime increases linearly with the input size.

Big O notation is a valuable tool for characterizing and comparing the efficiency of algorithms. It allows us to categorize algorithms based on their performance and scalability.

The key idea behind Big O notation is to focus on the dominant term or factor that contributes the most to an algorithm's resource consumption. This dominant term represents the worst-case scenario for the algorithm's performance.

For instance, if an algorithm's runtime is described by the expression $T(n) = 5n^2 + 3n + 2$, in Big O notation, it would be simplified to $O(n^2)$. This simplification discards the lower-order terms (3n and 2) and the constant factor (5) since they become less significant as the input size grows.

The concept of worst-case analysis is central to Big O notation. It assumes that the algorithm encounters the input that requires the maximum amount of resources, ensuring that the algorithm behaves efficiently under all conditions.

Big O notation is particularly useful for comparing algorithms that solve the same problem. By examining their time or space complexity in terms of Big O notation, we can identify which algorithm is more efficient for different input sizes.

Common time complexity classes described by Big O notation include $O(1)$ (constant time), $O(\log n)$ (logarithmic time), $O(n)$ (linear time), $O(n \log n)$ (linearithmic time), $O(n^2)$ (quadratic time), and more. These classes represent different growth rates of algorithms' resource requirements.

For example, an algorithm with a time complexity of $O(1)$ has a constant runtime regardless of the input size. This is ideal for scenarios where fast, predictable execution is essential.

In contrast, an algorithm with a time complexity of $O(n^2)$ experiences a quadratic increase in runtime with larger input sizes. This is less efficient and may be suitable for smaller datasets but not practical for larger ones.

Big O notation also extends to space complexity analysis, which quantifies an algorithm's memory usage. For example, an algorithm with a space complexity of $O(1)$ uses a constant amount of memory regardless of input size, while an algorithm with O(n) space complexity scales linearly with input size.

Efficient algorithms aim to minimize both time and space complexity, achieving a balance between computational speed and memory usage. However, optimizing one aspect may come at the expense of the other, and developers must make informed decisions based on the specific requirements of their applications.

In addition to worst-case analysis, Big O notation allows for best-case and average-case analysis. Best-case analysis focuses on the scenario where the algorithm performs optimally, while average-case analysis considers the expected performance over all possible inputs.

Best-case analysis can provide insights into an algorithm's potential, but it may not reflect its typical behavior in practice. Average-case analysis offers a more realistic view of an algorithm's performance, considering input distribution and probabilities.

While Big O notation is a powerful tool for algorithm analysis, it has its limitations. It provides an upper bound on the growth rate of an algorithm but does not account for constant factors, lower-order terms, or specific hardware optimizations.

Additionally, Big O notation provides a worst-case scenario analysis, which may not always reflect real-world conditions. For some applications, it may be more important to analyze average-case or best-case performance.

In practice, complexity analysis should be complemented by empirical testing and profiling in real-world scenarios to validate theoretical predictions.

Despite its limitations, Big O notation remains a fundamental concept in computer science and a valuable tool for algorithm design and evaluation.

It enables developers to make informed decisions about algorithm selection, optimization, and trade-offs, ensuring efficient resource utilization in various applications.

Efficient algorithms are at the core of many modern technologies, from web search engines and data processing to machine learning and artificial intelligence.

In summary, Big O notation is a mathematical tool used to describe the upper bound on the growth rate of an algorithm's resource requirements, such as time and space complexity. It simplifies complex expressions to focus on the dominant term, representing the algorithm's worst-case performance.

Time complexity classes like $O(1)$, $O(\log n)$, $O(n)$, and $O(n^2)$ categorize algorithms based on their growth rates, allowing for efficient algorithm comparison and selection.

Big O notation is also applicable to space complexity analysis, quantifying an algorithm's memory usage.

While Big O notation has limitations and simplifications, it plays a crucial role in algorithm design and analysis, helping developers create efficient solutions for a wide range of applications.

Chapter 4: Sorting and Searching Algorithms

Sorting algorithms are a fundamental topic in computer science, playing a crucial role in various applications and systems. At their core, sorting algorithms arrange a collection of elements in a specific order, often in ascending or descending order.

Sorting is a common operation in data processing, database management, and information retrieval. It's essential for organizing data in a way that facilitates efficient searching and analysis.

One of the simplest sorting algorithms is the "bubble sort." Bubble sort repeatedly steps through the list, compares adjacent elements, and swaps them if they are in the wrong order. This process continues until the entire list is sorted.

While bubble sort is easy to understand, it is not efficient for large datasets. Its time complexity can be as high as $O(n^2)$, making it impractical for sorting large lists.

Another simple sorting algorithm is the "insertion sort." Insertion sort builds the final sorted array one item at a time, taking each element from the input and inserting it into its correct position in the sorted array.

Insertion sort performs well for small datasets but becomes inefficient as the dataset size increases. Its time complexity is also $O(n^2)$ in the worst case.

"Selection sort" is yet another elementary sorting algorithm. Selection sort divides the input list into two parts: the left part contains the sorted elements, while the right part holds the unsorted elements. The algorithm repeatedly selects the smallest (or largest) element from the unsorted part and moves it to the sorted part.

Like bubble and insertion sorts, selection sort has a time complexity of O(n^2) in the worst case, making it less suitable for large datasets.

To improve sorting efficiency, more advanced algorithms are often used. One such algorithm is "merge sort."

Merge sort is a divide-and-conquer algorithm that splits the input into smaller sublists, recursively sorts them, and then merges the sorted sublists to produce a fully sorted list.

Merge sort has a time complexity of O(n log n), making it more efficient than the previous sorting algorithms for larger datasets. It is known for its stability, meaning that equal elements retain their relative order in the sorted output.

"Quick sort" is another efficient sorting algorithm, also based on the divide-and-conquer approach. Quick sort selects a "pivot" element from the input list and partitions the other elements into two sublists: one with elements less than the pivot and another with elements greater than the pivot. It then recursively sorts the sublists.

Quick sort is known for its speed and is often used in practice for its average-case time complexity of O(n log n). However, its worst-case time complexity can be O(n^2), which is a drawback in specific situations.

"Heap sort" is a comparison-based sorting algorithm that relies on a data structure called a "heap." A heap is a binary tree where each node satisfies the heap property, which means that a parent node has a value greater (or smaller) than its children.

Heap sort works by transforming the input list into a max-heap (for ascending order) or a min-heap (for descending order). It then repeatedly extracts the maximum (or minimum) element and rebuilds the heap until the entire list is sorted.

Heap sort has a time complexity of O(n log n) and is often used when a stable sort is not required.

Counting sort and radix sort are non-comparative sorting algorithms that take advantage of specific characteristics of the data. Counting sort, for example, is efficient for sorting integers within a bounded range.

Radix sort, on the other hand, sorts numbers by comparing their digits from right to left, starting with the least significant digit. It can be particularly efficient for sorting integers with a fixed number of digits.

Sorting algorithms are not limited to numerical data; they can be applied to various data types, including strings, objects, and more. The principles of sorting remain the same, but the comparison operation may differ depending on the data type.

In some scenarios, the choice of sorting algorithm can have a significant impact on performance. For small datasets or nearly sorted data, simple algorithms like insertion sort may outperform more complex ones.

However, for large datasets or data with unpredictable patterns, advanced sorting algorithms like merge sort or quick sort are preferred due to their efficient time complexity.

It's worth noting that some programming languages and libraries provide built-in sorting functions that handle the underlying details for developers. These built-in functions often use efficient sorting algorithms to ensure good performance.

Choosing the right sorting algorithm depends on the specific requirements of the task and the characteristics of the data. Developers must consider factors like dataset size, data distribution, and the need for stability when selecting a sorting algorithm.

In summary, sorting algorithms are essential tools in computer science and data processing. They enable the efficient organization of data, making it easier to search, analyze, and retrieve information.

From simple algorithms like bubble sort and insertion sort to more complex ones like merge sort and quick sort, various sorting techniques are available to suit different needs.

Understanding the characteristics and performance of sorting algorithms empowers developers to make informed decisions and optimize their applications for efficient data processing.

Searching is a fundamental operation in computer science and information retrieval, essential for finding specific data within a collection. Various searching techniques exist, each with its strengths, weaknesses, and use cases.

One of the simplest searching methods is linear search, also known as sequential search. Linear search iterates through a collection of elements one by one until it finds the target element or reaches the end of the collection.

Linear search is straightforward to implement but not the most efficient for large datasets. Its time complexity is $O(n)$, where n represents the number of elements in the collection.

Another common searching technique is binary search. Binary search is applicable to sorted collections, and it works by repeatedly dividing the search range in half, eliminating half of the remaining elements at each step.

Binary search has a time complexity of $O(\log n)$, making it much more efficient than linear search for large sorted datasets. It is often used in scenarios where the data is already sorted or can be sorted efficiently.

Hashing is another powerful searching technique that uses a data structure called a hash table. In a hash table, data is stored in key-value pairs, and a hash function is used to map keys to specific locations in the table.

Hashing allows for rapid data retrieval, as the hash function quickly determines where the desired data is stored. The time complexity for hash table operations is typically O(1) on average, making it highly efficient.

However, hash table performance can degrade if there are many hash collisions, where different keys map to the same location. To mitigate this, techniques like open addressing and chaining are used to handle collisions.

Tree-based searching techniques, such as binary search trees (BSTs) and balanced trees like AVL trees and Red-Black trees, are used to maintain sorted data efficiently. In a binary search tree, each node has at most two children, with elements in the left subtree being smaller than the node's value and elements in the right subtree being larger.

BSTs provide efficient searching with an average time complexity of O(log n) but can degrade to O(n) in the worst case if the tree is unbalanced. Balanced trees, like AVL and Red-Black trees, ensure that the tree remains balanced, guaranteeing efficient searching.

Ternary search trees (TSTs) are another tree-based data structure that combines elements of binary search trees and digital search tries. TSTs are particularly useful for searching within a dictionary or autocomplete functionality.

TSTs have a time complexity similar to binary search trees, typically O(log n) on average but may degrade to O(n) in the worst case if the tree is unbalanced.

Searching techniques also extend to text and pattern searching. One of the most well-known text searching algorithms is the Knuth-Morris-Pratt (KMP) algorithm, used for finding occurrences of a substring (pattern) within a longer text.

The KMP algorithm uses a preprocessing step to build a partial match table, allowing it to skip unnecessary comparisons during the search. This optimization results in a time complexity of O(n + m), where n is the length of the text and m is the length of the pattern.

The Boyer-Moore algorithm is another text searching algorithm that focuses on character comparisons and can provide efficient searching in practice.

It preprocesses the pattern and uses a "bad character" table to skip ahead when a mismatch occurs, leading to an average-case time complexity of O(n/m) for searching.

Regular expressions, or regex, provide a powerful way to search for patterns in text. Regex patterns are defined using a specific syntax that allows for complex pattern matching.

While regex searching can be highly flexible, it may not be the most efficient choice for some tasks due to its computational complexity, which can vary depending on the pattern and input text.

Pattern searching is crucial in many applications, including text editors, search engines, and data analysis tools. The choice of a searching technique depends on factors like the nature of the data, the type of search query, and the expected dataset size.

Efficiency considerations are essential when selecting a searching technique. For example, binary search is ideal for large sorted datasets, while hashing is excellent for fast data retrieval from unsorted collections.

Balanced trees strike a balance between sorting and searching efficiency, making them suitable for various scenarios.

When dealing with text and patterns, specialized algorithms like KMP and Boyer-Moore excel in substring and pattern matching.

It's worth noting that practical searching often involves a combination of techniques. For instance, a database management system may use indexing structures like B-trees or hash tables for efficient data retrieval and then apply additional filtering or pattern matching for specific queries.

In summary, searching techniques are essential tools in computer science and data processing, enabling efficient data retrieval and pattern matching.

Various searching methods, including linear search, binary search, hashing, and tree-based structures, offer different trade-offs in terms of time and space complexity.

Choosing the right searching technique depends on the specific requirements of the task, the nature of the data, and the expected dataset size.

Efficiency considerations play a crucial role in selecting the most appropriate searching method, ensuring that data retrieval and pattern matching are performed quickly and effectively in various applications.

Chapter 5: Dynamic Programming and Greedy Techniques

Dynamic programming is a powerful problem-solving technique that is widely used in computer science and mathematics. It is particularly valuable for solving optimization problems and combinatorial problems efficiently.

Dynamic programming is not a specific algorithm but rather a general approach to solving problems by breaking them down into smaller subproblems. The key idea is to solve each subproblem only once and store its result to avoid redundant calculations.

This technique is especially useful when a problem can be decomposed into overlapping subproblems, which means that the same subproblem is encountered multiple times during the solution process.

One of the fundamental characteristics of dynamic programming is the concept of memoization. Memoization involves storing the results of expensive function calls and returning the cached result when the same inputs occur again.

Dynamic programming is applicable to a wide range of problems, including those in computer science, operations research, and economics. It is a common approach for optimizing algorithms and finding the most efficient solutions.

The term "dynamic programming" was coined by Richard Bellman in the 1950s while working on problems related to optimal control processes. Despite the name, dynamic programming is not limited to dynamic problems but is a general methodology for solving optimization problems.

One of the most well-known examples of dynamic programming is the Fibonacci sequence. The Fibonacci sequence is a sequence of numbers where each number is the sum of the two preceding ones.

A naive recursive approach to calculating Fibonacci numbers would involve redundant calculations, as many subproblems are solved multiple times.

However, by using dynamic programming and memoization, you can calculate Fibonacci numbers efficiently with a time complexity of $O(n)$, where n is the desired Fibonacci number.

The dynamic programming approach involves breaking down the problem into smaller subproblems and solving them bottom-up. In the case of Fibonacci numbers, you start with the base cases (F(0) and F(1)), compute F(2), F(3), and so on, until you reach the desired Fibonacci number.

The memoization technique ensures that you store the results of previously calculated Fibonacci numbers, preventing redundant calculations.

Dynamic programming can be categorized into two main types: top-down and bottom-up.

Top-down dynamic programming, also known as memoization, starts with the original problem and breaks it down into smaller subproblems. It then recursively solves each subproblem and caches the results.

Bottom-up dynamic programming, on the other hand, starts with the smallest subproblems and builds up to the original problem. It typically uses an array or table to store the results of subproblems and fills it iteratively.

Both top-down and bottom-up approaches have their advantages and are suitable for different scenarios.

Dynamic programming is often used to solve optimization problems, where the goal is to find the best solution among a set of possible solutions. Examples of optimization problems include finding the shortest path in a graph, minimizing the cost of a task, or maximizing profit.

One classic example of dynamic programming is the Knapsack problem. In the Knapsack problem, you have a set of items, each with a weight and a value, and a knapsack with a limited weight capacity. The goal is to select a combination of items to maximize their total value while staying within the knapsack's weight limit.

Dynamic programming provides an efficient solution to the Knapsack problem, where the subproblems involve deciding whether to include each item in the knapsack or not.

Another well-known problem that dynamic programming can solve is the Longest Common Subsequence (LCS) problem. In the LCS problem, you are given two sequences of elements, and the goal is to find the longest subsequence that appears in both sequences.

Dynamic programming can be used to find the LCS efficiently by breaking down the problem into smaller subproblems and finding the LCS of prefixes of the sequences.

The application of dynamic programming extends beyond traditional computer science problems. It is also used in diverse fields such as natural language processing, bioinformatics, and economics.

For example, in natural language processing, dynamic programming algorithms are employed for tasks like text alignment and parsing.

In bioinformatics, dynamic programming is used for sequence alignment, which is essential for comparing DNA or protein sequences.

Economists use dynamic programming to model decision-making processes and optimize resource allocation in various economic scenarios.

Dynamic programming is a versatile technique with a broad range of applications, and its efficiency in solving optimization problems makes it a valuable tool in computer science and beyond.

While dynamic programming can be a powerful approach, it is essential to recognize when it is suitable for a problem. Not all problems benefit from dynamic programming, and using it for simple or non-optimization problems may result in unnecessary complexity.

In summary, dynamic programming is a problem-solving technique that breaks down complex problems into smaller subproblems and efficiently solves them. It is particularly useful for optimization problems and problems with overlapping subproblems.

Dynamic programming can be applied in various domains, from computer science to natural language processing and economics. It offers both top-down (memoization) and bottom-up approaches to problem-solving.

Choosing the right approach depends on the problem at hand, and understanding the principles of dynamic programming is crucial for effective problem-solving and optimization.

Greedy algorithms are a class of problem-solving techniques that make a series of choices at each step with the hope of finding the overall best solution. The key characteristic of greedy algorithms is their reliance on making the locally optimal choice at each step, hoping that it will lead to a globally optimal solution.

This approach is particularly useful when solving optimization problems where you want to find the best solution among a set of possible solutions. Greedy algorithms are often easy to understand and implement, making them a valuable tool in various domains of computer science and beyond.

One classic example of a problem that can be solved using a greedy algorithm is the "coin change" problem. In this problem, you are given a set of coin denominations and a target amount to make using the fewest coins possible.

The greedy approach involves selecting the largest coin denomination that does not exceed the remaining amount at each step. This continues until the target amount is reached.

The greedy algorithm for the coin change problem is efficient and provides an optimal solution when coin denominations are in a specific format, such as U.S. coin denominations (quarters, dimes, nickels, and pennies).

However, it's important to note that the greedy algorithm may not always yield the optimal solution for every set of coin denominations.

In some cases, a different set of coin denominations could result in the greedy algorithm providing a suboptimal solution.

This highlights a key characteristic of greedy algorithms: they are not guaranteed to find the globally optimal solution for all instances of a problem.

Despite this limitation, greedy algorithms are widely used in various scenarios where they do provide the optimal or near-optimal solution.

Another example of a problem well-suited for a greedy approach is the "activity selection" problem. In this problem, you are given a set of activities, each with a start time and an end time, and the goal is to select the maximum number of non-overlapping activities.

The greedy algorithm for activity selection involves sorting the activities by their end times and then selecting them one by one in ascending order of end times.

This approach ensures that the selected activities do not overlap and maximizes the number of chosen activities.

Greedy algorithms are not limited to problems involving numbers or sequences; they can be applied to a wide range of optimization problems.

In the "Huffman coding" algorithm, a greedy approach is used to compress data efficiently. Huffman coding assigns variable-length codes to characters in a way that shorter codes are given to more frequent characters, resulting in optimal compression for a given set of data.

The greedy choice in Huffman coding is to merge the two least frequent characters into a new composite character and repeat this process until only one character remains.

Greedy algorithms are also employed in various scheduling and optimization problems. For example, in the "job scheduling" problem, where you have a set of jobs with deadlines and profits, the greedy approach involves selecting jobs in descending order of profit and scheduling them if their deadlines allow.

Similarly, in the "knapsack" problem, where you have a set of items with weights and values and a knapsack with a limited capacity, the greedy approach involves selecting items in descending order of value-to-weight ratio until the knapsack is full.

While greedy algorithms are powerful tools, it's crucial to be aware of their limitations. They do not guarantee the globally optimal solution for all problems, and their success often depends on the problem's specific characteristics.

In some cases, proving the correctness of a greedy algorithm and demonstrating that it consistently provides the optimal solution can be challenging.

To determine if a greedy algorithm is appropriate for a particular problem, it's essential to consider the problem's structure and characteristics.

Greedy algorithms work well when the problem exhibits the "greedy choice property," meaning that making the locally optimal choice at each step leads to a globally optimal solution.

They also work well when the problem has "optimal substructure," which means that the optimal solution to the overall problem can be constructed from optimal solutions to its subproblems.

In summary, greedy algorithms are a valuable class of problem-solving techniques that prioritize locally optimal choices in the hope of finding a globally optimal solution. They are widely used in various domains, including coin change, activity selection, Huffman coding, job scheduling, and knapsack problems.

While not guaranteed to find the globally optimal solution for all instances of a problem, greedy algorithms are often efficient and provide optimal or near-optimal solutions in many practical scenarios.

Understanding the problem's structure and characteristics is essential for determining whether a greedy algorithm is suitable and for effectively applying this approach to optimization problems.

Chapter 6: Navigating Graphs and Networks

Graph theory is a branch of mathematics that focuses on the study of graphs, which are mathematical structures used to model relationships between objects. A graph consists of a set of vertices (or nodes) and a set of edges (or arcs) that connect pairs of vertices.

Graphs can be used to represent a wide range of real-world systems and phenomena, making graph theory a fundamental and versatile field with applications in various disciplines.

The study of graphs dates back to the 18th century, and the field has since developed into a rich and diverse area of mathematics.

Graphs can be classified into different types based on their characteristics and properties.

One common classification is based on the presence or absence of direction in edges. In an undirected graph, edges have no direction, meaning they connect vertices without a specific order.

Conversely, in a directed graph (or digraph), edges have a direction, indicating a one-way relationship from one vertex to another.

Graphs can also be categorized based on whether or not they allow multiple edges between the same pair of vertices. In simple graphs, no more than one edge is allowed between any two vertices.

However, in multigraphs, multiple edges between the same vertices are permitted, each with potentially different properties.

Graphs can further be classified based on whether or not they allow loops, which are edges that connect a vertex to itself. In simple graphs, loops are not allowed, while in pseudographs, loops are permitted.

Another important distinction is between connected and disconnected graphs. A connected graph is one where there is a path between any pair of vertices, while a disconnected graph consists of two or more isolated components.

Graph theory provides a framework for describing and analyzing various relationships and structures in both the natural and human-made world.

For example, in social networks, vertices represent individuals, and edges represent connections or friendships between them. Analyzing the structure of social networks using graph theory can reveal patterns of influence, information flow, and community structure.

In transportation networks, vertices represent locations, and edges represent the physical links or roads between them. Graph theory can be used to optimize routes, analyze traffic flow, and plan efficient transportation systems.

In computer science, graphs are used to model data structures and relationships between data points. Data structures like trees and linked lists can be seen as specialized forms of graphs, and algorithms for graph traversal and searching are fundamental to computer science.

One of the essential concepts in graph theory is the degree of a vertex, which is the number of edges incident to it. In an undirected graph, the degree of a vertex is simply the count of edges connected to it.

In a directed graph, vertices have both in-degrees (the number of incoming edges) and out-degrees (the number of outgoing edges).

The concept of degree is crucial in analyzing the connectivity and structure of a graph. For example, in an undirected graph, if every vertex has an even degree, it is possible to find a path that traverses every edge without retracing any.

On the other hand, if there are exactly two vertices with odd degrees, it is possible to find a path that starts and ends at those vertices, visiting each edge exactly once (an Eulerian path).

Graph theory also deals with the concept of a cycle, which is a path that starts and ends at the same vertex. In an undirected graph, a cycle is a closed path that visits each vertex and edge exactly once (an Eulerian cycle).

In a directed graph, cycles can be more complex, as they must follow the direction of edges. Cycles are fundamental in graph theory, and understanding their properties is essential for various applications.

Another important concept in graph theory is connectivity. A graph is considered connected if there is a path between any pair of its vertices. If a graph is not connected, it consists of separate connected components.

Graphs can be used to represent various real-world problems and solve them efficiently.

One classic example is the traveling salesman problem (TSP), where a salesman needs to find the shortest route that visits a set of cities and returns to the starting city. TSP can be modeled as a graph, where cities are vertices, and edges represent distances between them.

Graph algorithms, such as Dijkstra's algorithm and the A* search algorithm, are used in route planning and navigation systems to find the shortest path between two locations in a network.

Graph theory also plays a crucial role in network analysis, such as finding the most influential nodes in a social network or identifying bottlenecks in a transportation network.

In computer science, graph algorithms are fundamental for tasks like searching, sorting, and traversing data structures, such as trees and linked lists.

Graph theory provides a rich set of tools and concepts for modeling and solving complex problems across various domains.

In summary, graph theory is a branch of mathematics that deals with the study of graphs, which are mathematical structures used to model relationships between objects. Graphs consist of vertices (nodes) and edges (arcs), and they can be directed or undirected, connected or disconnected, and have various properties and characteristics.

Graph theory has wide-ranging applications in fields such as social networks, transportation systems, computer science, and network analysis. It provides essential concepts, such as degrees, cycles, and connectivity, for analyzing and solving problems represented as graphs.

The study of graph theory continues to be an active and evolving field with ongoing research and applications in diverse areas of science and technology.

Graph traversal and finding shortest paths are fundamental operations in graph theory with wide-ranging applications in various fields. These operations involve navigating through a graph, which is a collection of vertices and edges, to explore relationships and optimize routes.

One of the most common algorithms for graph traversal is Depth-First Search (DFS). DFS explores as far as possible along each branch before backtracking, making it particularly useful for tasks like maze solving, topological sorting, and cycle detection.

The DFS algorithm starts at an initial vertex and explores adjacent vertices by following one branch until it reaches a dead-end or encounters a vertex already visited. When a dead-end is reached or all adjacent vertices have been visited, DFS backtracks to the previous vertex and continues exploring other branches.

DFS can be implemented using either recursion or an explicit stack data structure. The order in which vertices are visited in DFS depends on the choice of the starting vertex and the specific implementation.

Another widely used graph traversal algorithm is Breadth-First Search (BFS). BFS explores all neighbors of a vertex before moving on to their neighbors, making it suitable for tasks like finding the shortest path in an unweighted graph, solving puzzles with multiple solutions, and network routing.

The BFS algorithm starts at an initial vertex and explores its neighbors first. Then, it visits the neighbors' neighbors, and so on, ensuring that vertices are visited in increasing order of distance from the starting vertex.

BFS can be implemented using a queue data structure, where vertices are enqueued and dequeued in a first-in-first-out (FIFO) order. The order in which vertices are visited in BFS guarantees that the shortest path from the starting vertex to any other vertex is discovered first.

Shortest path algorithms aim to find the most efficient route between two vertices in a graph. The choice of algorithm depends on the type of graph (weighted or unweighted) and specific requirements.

In unweighted graphs, where all edges have the same weight or cost, BFS can be used to find the shortest path. This is because BFS guarantees that the first time a vertex is reached, it is reached via the shortest path.

However, in weighted graphs, where edges have different costs or weights, more specialized algorithms are needed. One such algorithm is Dijkstra's algorithm, which finds the shortest path in a weighted, directed or undirected graph with non-negative edge weights.

Dijkstra's algorithm maintains a priority queue of vertices to explore and updates the tentative distances to each vertex. It repeatedly selects the vertex with the smallest tentative distance, explores its neighbors, and updates their distances if a shorter path is found.

Dijkstra's algorithm is efficient for finding shortest paths in graphs with non-negative edge weights but may not work correctly in the presence of negative edge weights.

In graphs with negative edge weights, the Bellman-Ford algorithm can be used to find the shortest path. The Bellman-Ford algorithm works for both weighted and unweighted graphs and can handle graphs with negative edge weights, provided they do not create negative weight cycles.

The Bellman-Ford algorithm initializes the distances to all vertices as infinity and gradually relaxes edges, reducing the distance estimates. It iteratively relaxes all edges until no further improvements can be made or a negative weight cycle is detected.

Another important algorithm for finding shortest paths is the Floyd-Warshall algorithm. The Floyd-Warshall algorithm computes the shortest path between all pairs of vertices in a weighted graph, allowing efficient query of shortest paths between any two vertices.

The algorithm uses dynamic programming to build a matrix of shortest path distances between all pairs of vertices. It iteratively considers all vertices as potential intermediaries in the shortest path and updates the matrix accordingly.

The Floyd-Warshall algorithm works for graphs with both positive and negative edge weights but cannot handle negative weight cycles.

In some cases, finding the single shortest path is not enough, and there is a need to find multiple shortest paths. One way to do this is to use algorithms like A* search or D* Lite, which find the shortest path from a starting vertex to a goal vertex while taking into account a heuristic that estimates the remaining cost.

A* search uses a priority queue to explore vertices, considering both the actual cost from the start and the estimated cost to the goal. It is commonly used in pathfinding and navigation systems, such as GPS routing and video games.

D* Lite is an improvement of A* search designed for dynamic environments where the graph may change over time. It efficiently updates the shortest path when edge costs or vertex states change, making it suitable for robotics and autonomous systems.

Graph traversal and shortest path algorithms have numerous applications in various domains, including network routing, transportation planning, social network analysis, and computer graphics.

For example, in network routing, algorithms like Dijkstra's and A* search help find the optimal routes for data packets in computer networks.

In transportation planning, these algorithms are used to optimize routes for vehicles, such as GPS navigation systems providing real-time traffic information.

In social network analysis, graph traversal algorithms help identify influential nodes and communities within a network, aiding in understanding information flow and social dynamics.

In computer graphics, shortest path algorithms are used for pathfinding in video games and simulating realistic movement in virtual environments.

These algorithms continue to be a critical part of computer science and are essential tools for solving a wide range of problems involving graphs and networks.

Chapter 7: Divide and Conquer Strategies

The divide and conquer approach is a powerful problem-solving technique used in computer science and mathematics. It involves breaking down a complex problem into smaller, more manageable subproblems, solving them independently, and then combining their solutions to solve the original problem.

The divide and conquer strategy is based on the idea of recursion, where a problem is divided into smaller instances of the same problem. Each smaller instance is solved using the same algorithm until a base case is reached, at which point the solutions are combined to produce the final result.

One classic example of the divide and conquer approach is the binary search algorithm. In binary search, a sorted list is divided into two halves, and the search is narrowed down to one of the halves based on whether the target value is greater or less than the middle element. This process is repeated until the target is found or the search range is empty.

Another well-known application of divide and conquer is the merge sort algorithm. Merge sort divides an unsorted list into smaller sublists, recursively sorts each sublist, and then merges the sorted sublists back together to produce a sorted list. The merge step is where the solutions of the subproblems are combined.

The divide and conquer approach is especially useful when solving problems with a recursive structure, such as those involving trees and graphs. For example, in tree traversal algorithms like in-order, pre-order, or post-order traversal, the divide and conquer strategy is applied to the left and right subtrees of a node.

In the context of computational complexity, the divide and conquer approach can often lead to more efficient algorithms compared to naive or brute-force solutions. By reducing the problem size at each step, divide and conquer algorithms can achieve better time and space complexity.

One of the key aspects of the divide and conquer approach is ensuring that the subproblems are independent and that their solutions can be combined correctly. This requires careful design of the algorithm and consideration of how the solutions of subproblems can be merged to solve the overall problem.

In some cases, divide and conquer algorithms may also involve conquering intermediate subproblems before reaching the final solution. This can lead to more complex recursive structures, such as the case of quicksort, where partitions are conquered before merging.

Divide and conquer is not limited to sorting and searching algorithms but can be applied to a wide range of problems. For instance, it is used in algorithms for fast Fourier transforms (FFT), matrix multiplication, and finding the closest pair of points in a two-dimensional plane.

In FFT, a complex problem of polynomial multiplication is divided into smaller problems by evaluating the polynomials at specific points, solving the subproblems, and then combining the results using interpolation.

Matrix multiplication using the Strassen algorithm is another example where divide and conquer is applied. In this algorithm, large matrices are divided into smaller submatrices, and the multiplication is performed using recursive calls and matrix additions.

The closest pair of points problem involves dividing a set of points into two halves, finding the closest pair of points in each half, and then merging the solutions by considering points that are close to the dividing line.

The divide and conquer approach is not without its challenges. One common issue is the need for additional space to store intermediate results and recursion stacks. Care must be taken to optimize memory usage and avoid excessive overhead.

Additionally, the choice of how to divide the problem and how to merge the solutions can significantly impact the efficiency of the algorithm. Designing an efficient divide and conquer algorithm often requires a deep understanding of the problem's structure and characteristics.

In summary, the divide and conquer approach is a fundamental problem-solving technique in computer science and mathematics. It involves breaking down complex problems into smaller, independent subproblems, solving them recursively, and then combining their solutions to solve the original problem efficiently.

Divide and conquer algorithms are used in a wide range of applications, including sorting, searching, tree traversal, matrix multiplication, and many other computational tasks.

While the approach offers significant advantages in terms of efficiency and elegance, it also poses challenges in terms of memory usage and algorithm design. Mastering the divide and conquer strategy is essential for computer scientists and mathematicians seeking to solve complex problems effectively.

Recursive problem-solving techniques are a fundamental concept in computer science and mathematics, enabling the elegant and efficient solution of various complex problems. These techniques rely on a process of breaking down a problem into smaller, more manageable instances of the same problem, and then solving those smaller instances recursively.

Recursion is a powerful concept that is based on the idea of self-reference, where a problem is solved by reducing it to smaller, similar subproblems. To apply recursion effectively, one needs to understand its principles, design recursive algorithms, and identify base cases that stop the recursion.

One classic example of recursive problem solving is the computation of factorials. A factorial of a non-negative integer n, denoted as n!, is the product of all positive integers from 1 to n. The recursive definition of the factorial function is n! = n * (n-1)!, where the base case is defined as 0! = 1.

In this recursive definition, the problem of computing n! is broken down into the problem of computing (n-1)!. The base case ensures that the recursion stops when n reaches 0, and the smaller instances are solved by recursively computing (n-1)!.

Another well-known example is the Fibonacci sequence, which is a series of numbers where each number is the sum of the two preceding ones (starting with 0 and 1). The nth Fibonacci number, denoted as F(n), can be defined recursively as F(n) = F(n-1) + F(n-2), with base cases F(0) = 0 and F(1) = 1.

In this recursive definition, the computation of F(n) is divided into two smaller instances: F(n-1) and F(n-2). Again, base cases are provided to halt the recursion when n reaches 0 or 1.

Recursion is not limited to mathematical problems; it has widespread applications in computer science and programming. One of the most common uses of recursion is in tree and graph traversal algorithms.

For example, consider a binary tree where each node has a left and right child. A recursive algorithm for in-order tree traversal would visit the left subtree, then the current node, and finally the right subtree. This process continues recursively for each subtree.

In this case, the problem of traversing the entire tree is divided into the problems of traversing the left subtree and the right subtree. The base case is reached when a null (empty) subtree is encountered, and the recursion stops.

Recursion also plays a crucial role in solving problems related to data structures, such as linked lists. For instance, reversing a linked list can be accomplished through a recursive approach, where the problem of reversing a list is reduced to reversing the rest of the list recursively.

The effectiveness of recursion lies in its ability to simplify complex problems by breaking them down into smaller, more manageable parts. However, it is essential to be cautious when using recursion, as improper use can lead to stack overflow errors and inefficient algorithms.

To use recursion effectively, it's crucial to ensure that each recursive call moves towards the base case, guaranteeing that the recursion will eventually terminate. Additionally, problems that can be solved more efficiently using iterative techniques should not be unnecessarily solved recursively.

Recursive problem-solving techniques are not limited to basic mathematical operations or tree traversals. They can be applied to a wide range of problems, from combinatorial problems like generating permutations and combinations to more complex tasks such as solving mazes, finding the shortest path in graphs, and optimizing resource allocation.

In computer science, recursive algorithms often exhibit elegant and concise code, making them a preferred choice for solving problems with recursive structures. However, it is essential to strike a balance between elegance and efficiency, as recursive algorithms may have higher memory and time complexity compared to their iterative counterparts.

In summary, recursive problem-solving techniques are a fundamental concept in computer science and mathematics. They involve breaking down complex problems into smaller, similar subproblems and solving them recursively, relying on self-reference and base cases to ensure termination.

Recursion is a powerful tool that can simplify problem-solving, especially for tasks with recursive structures like trees and graphs. However, it should be used judiciously, considering both elegance and efficiency, to avoid potential pitfalls and ensure optimal solutions.

Chapter 8: Advanced Data Structures and Applications

Specialized data structures are a critical component of efficient algorithm design, enabling the optimization of various computational tasks. These data structures are tailored to specific types of problems and operations, offering advantages in terms of time and space complexity.

One such specialized data structure is the heap, which is commonly used in priority queue operations. A heap is a tree-based structure where each node satisfies the heap property, ensuring that the parent node has a higher (or lower) priority than its children, depending on whether it's a max-heap or a min-heap.

The heap data structure is particularly efficient for tasks that require frequent insertion and removal of elements with the highest (or lowest) priority. For example, heaps are commonly used in algorithms like Dijkstra's shortest path and Prim's minimum spanning tree to efficiently select the next element to process.

Another specialized data structure is the hash table, which provides fast access to data based on a key-value pair. Hash tables use a hash function to map keys to specific locations in an array, allowing for constant-time average-case retrieval, insertion, and deletion operations.

Hash tables are widely used in tasks where quick data access is crucial, such as implementing dictionaries, caching systems, and symbol tables in programming languages. They offer a balance between time and space complexity, making them a preferred choice for many applications.

Trie (pronounced "try") is another specialized data structure used for efficient storage and retrieval of strings. Tries are tree-like structures where each node represents a character in a string, and paths from the root to the leaves spell out words.

Tries are commonly employed in tasks like autocomplete suggestions, spell checkers, and searching for strings with common prefixes. They excel at reducing time complexity for operations involving large datasets of words or strings.

Specialized data structures can also be optimized for spatial data and geometrical problems. Quadtree and octree are examples of such structures, which partition two-dimensional and three-dimensional space, respectively, into hierarchical regions.

Quadtree is used in tasks like image compression, collision detection in computer graphics, and geographic information systems (GIS). It allows for efficient spatial indexing and search operations.

Similarly, octrees are employed in three-dimensional graphics, scientific simulations, and computational geometry for tasks like ray tracing, spatial subdivision, and nearest neighbor queries in 3D space.

Segment trees and interval trees are specialized data structures designed for handling intervals or segments of data. A segment tree efficiently stores and queries segments of data, such as intervals or ranges.

Interval trees, on the other hand, are specialized for efficient searching of intervals that overlap with a given query interval. These data structures are commonly used in applications involving time intervals, scheduling, and database indexing.

Fenwick tree, also known as a binary indexed tree (BIT), is a specialized data structure for efficient range queries and updates on an array of values. It is particularly well-suited for tasks like cumulative frequency calculations and dynamic prefix sums.

Bloom filters are specialized data structures used to test whether an element is a member of a set. They use multiple hash functions to represent elements and can efficiently determine membership, but they may produce false positives.

Bloom filters are commonly employed in tasks like spell checking, database query optimization, and web caching to quickly eliminate unnecessary work based on probable membership.

Splay tree is a self-adjusting binary search tree designed to optimize frequently accessed elements. It rearranges nodes to bring frequently accessed items closer to the root, reducing access time for frequently used elements.

Splay trees are used in applications where certain items are accessed more frequently than others, such as caching mechanisms and dynamic search structures.

Treap is another specialized data structure that combines the properties of a binary search tree (BST) and a heap. It assigns a random priority to each node while maintaining the BST property, ensuring that the tree remains balanced on average.

Treaps are utilized in tasks where the order of insertion matters but balanced tree structures are necessary for efficient operations, such as randomized sorting and data stream processing.

Skip list is a versatile data structure that offers logarithmic time complexity for search, insertion, and deletion operations, similar to balanced trees but with simpler implementation. Skip lists consist of multiple linked lists at different levels, allowing for efficient traversal and modification.

Skip lists are used in various applications, including data indexing, dictionary implementations, and database management systems.

Each specialized data structure mentioned here has its unique advantages and is optimized for specific types of problems and operations. The choice of data structure depends on the requirements of the task at hand, balancing factors such as time complexity, space complexity, and ease of implementation.

Understanding these specialized data structures and their characteristics is essential for computer scientists and programmers when designing efficient algorithms and solving real-world computational problems efficiently.

Advanced data structures play a pivotal role in solving complex real-world problems across various domains. These data structures are specifically designed to address specific challenges in specific applications, providing efficient solutions to a wide range of computational tasks.

In the realm of databases and information retrieval, B-trees are a critical data structure. B-trees are balanced tree structures that excel at indexing large volumes of data, making them ideal for database management systems and file systems. Their balanced nature ensures that search, insertion, and deletion operations have logarithmic time complexity, making them efficient for handling massive datasets.

Spatial data applications, such as geographic information systems (GIS) and mapping software, often rely on specialized data structures like R-trees. R-trees are designed for efficient indexing of spatial objects, allowing for fast retrieval and querying of geographical data. They are used in tasks like finding nearby locations, identifying overlapping regions, and optimizing route planning.

In computer graphics and rendering, kd-trees are a valuable tool. These trees are used for efficiently finding the nearest neighbor and intersecting objects in three-dimensional space. Kd-trees are essential in ray tracing algorithms, collision detection, and 3D modeling software, where rapid spatial queries are required for realistic rendering.

Sparse matrices, which store mostly zero values, are a specialized data structure used in scientific computing and numerical simulations. Compressed sparse row (CSR) and compressed sparse column (CSC) formats are two common representations for sparse matrices. They are employed in tasks such as solving linear systems of equations, finite element analysis, and network analysis, where memory efficiency is crucial.

Graph databases leverage advanced data structures like property graphs and triple stores to manage complex relationships and semistructured data. These databases are employed in applications involving social networks, recommendation systems, and knowledge graphs, where the relationships between entities are as important as the entities themselves.

Bloom filters, which use hash functions to test for set membership, find applications in network routers and caching systems. They help quickly identify whether an element is present in a large dataset, allowing routers to make informed routing decisions and caches to reduce unnecessary data retrieval.

Suffix trees and suffix arrays are essential in natural language processing and string matching. They enable efficient pattern matching in large texts, facilitating tasks like searching for keywords in search engines, identifying plagiarism in documents, and analyzing DNA sequences for bioinformatics research.

In data compression, Huffman trees are used to create variable-length codes for encoding data more efficiently. Huffman coding reduces the size of data by assigning shorter codes to more frequent symbols, making it a fundamental technique in file compression formats like ZIP and JPEG.

In concurrent and parallel programming, lock-free data structures and concurrent data structures are crucial for building high-performance applications. They ensure that multiple threads can access shared data without the need for locks, leading to improved scalability and reduced contention. Applications include real-time systems, financial trading platforms, and gaming engines.

For internet security, cryptographic data structures like Merkle trees and hash chains are used to ensure data integrity. These data structures enable secure verification of data by comparing hashes, making them vital in blockchain technology, digital signatures, and certificate authorities.

In computer networks, data structures like tries are used for efficient routing and IP address lookups. Tries provide a hierarchical structure for organizing IP address prefixes, enabling routers to make quick routing decisions in large-scale networks.

Advanced data structures are also applied in artificial intelligence and machine learning. KD-trees and ball trees, for instance, are used in nearest neighbor search algorithms to find similar data points in high-dimensional spaces. These structures are employed in recommendation systems, image recognition, and anomaly detection.

Graph algorithms, such as Dijkstra's algorithm and A* search, are fundamental in route planning applications, including GPS navigation and logistics optimization. These algorithms find the shortest paths between locations, minimizing travel time and fuel consumption.

Cuckoo hashing is utilized in modern data storage systems, ensuring efficient key-value storage and retrieval. It offers constant-time average-case performance for insertion, deletion, and lookup operations and is employed in in-memory databases, distributed storage, and distributed hash tables (DHTs).

In summary, advanced data structures are indispensable in addressing complex real-world challenges across various fields. Their specialized designs provide efficient solutions to problems ranging from large-scale data management and spatial queries to network routing, security, and artificial intelligence.

These data structures enable organizations to optimize their systems, improve data processing speed, reduce memory usage, and enhance the overall efficiency of computational tasks. Understanding the principles and applications of advanced data structures is essential for engineers, computer scientists, and developers working on cutting-edge technology and tackling real-world problems.

Chapter 9: Algorithmic Challenges and Complex Problems

Handling algorithmic challenges is a central aspect of computer science and programming, requiring problem-solving skills and a deep understanding of data structures and algorithms. These challenges encompass a wide range of complexities, from basic to advanced, and arise in various domains, from software development to scientific research.

One common challenge is optimizing time complexity, which involves finding ways to make algorithms faster and more efficient. Efficiency is crucial, as it directly impacts the performance of software applications and the user experience. Algorithmic efficiency often involves reducing unnecessary operations, minimizing data traversal, and selecting appropriate data structures.

Another challenge is managing space complexity, which involves efficiently using memory resources. Space-efficient algorithms and data structures are essential for applications with limited memory, such as embedded systems and mobile devices. Achieving low space complexity often requires clever techniques like data compression and dynamic memory management.

Handling large datasets is a common challenge in data science and analytics. Efficient algorithms for processing and analyzing big data are essential in fields like machine learning, data mining, and bioinformatics. Optimizing data storage, retrieval, and computation becomes critical when working with massive amounts of information.

Algorithmic challenges also arise in the context of real-time systems, where algorithms must meet strict timing constraints. These systems are prevalent in areas like robotics, autonomous vehicles, and aviation, where algorithms must make split-second decisions. Meeting real-time requirements often involves careful algorithm design and analysis to ensure that computations complete within specified time bounds.

Dealing with dynamic data structures is another challenge, as data can change in size and shape over time. Algorithms must adapt to these changes efficiently, whether it's in the context of resizing arrays, handling dynamic graphs, or maintaining balanced trees. Dynamic data structures are essential in databases, network protocols, and interactive applications.

Parallelism and concurrency present significant algorithmic challenges. Modern computer systems often have multiple cores or processors, enabling parallel execution of tasks. Developing algorithms that can take advantage of parallelism while avoiding race conditions and deadlocks is a complex task. Parallel algorithms are crucial for scientific simulations, multimedia processing, and high-performance computing.

Handling algorithmic challenges also includes solving optimization problems, where the goal is to find the best solution among many possible alternatives. These problems are common in logistics, scheduling, and resource allocation, where algorithms must balance conflicting objectives to achieve optimal outcomes. Optimization algorithms range from simple greedy approaches to sophisticated metaheuristics.

Dealing with uncertainty and randomness is a challenge in probabilistic algorithms. These algorithms use randomness to make decisions or provide approximate solutions to problems. They find applications in cryptography, Monte Carlo simulations, and machine learning, where randomness can improve efficiency or provide privacy.

Complexity theory addresses the fundamental limits of computation and the classification of problems based on their computational difficulty. Understanding the computational complexity of problems is crucial for algorithm design, as it helps identify problems that are likely to be intractable and those that can be solved efficiently. Complexity theory also provides tools for proving the hardness of problems, which is essential in cryptography and security.

In some cases, algorithms must handle adversarial inputs, where an adversary tries to manipulate the system to its advantage. Adversarial scenarios are prevalent in cybersecurity, where algorithms must defend against attacks and ensure the integrity and confidentiality of data. Designing algorithms that are robust to adversarial inputs is a critical challenge.

Algorithmic challenges also encompass ethical considerations. Algorithms can have significant societal impacts, and designers must consider fairness, bias, transparency, and accountability in algorithmic decision-making. Addressing these challenges involves developing algorithms that are ethically responsible and ensuring that they do not discriminate or harm vulnerable populations.

Handling algorithmic challenges requires a systematic approach to problem solving. Engineers and computer scientists often follow a structured process that includes problem formulation, algorithm design, implementation, testing, and optimization. They use a variety of tools and techniques, such as pseudocode, flowcharts, and UML diagrams, to visualize and communicate their algorithms.

Algorithmic challenges are not limited to the realm of computer science. They also arise in mathematics, physics, biology, and other scientific disciplines. Scientists use algorithms to model complex systems, simulate physical phenomena, analyze experimental data, and make predictions.

In research and academia, algorithmic challenges drive innovation and push the boundaries of knowledge. Researchers explore new algorithmic techniques, develop novel data structures, and prove theorems about the computational complexity of problems. Their work contributes to advances in artificial intelligence, robotics, and computational science.

Handling algorithmic challenges is a continuous process of learning and adaptation. Technology evolves rapidly, and new challenges emerge as computing power increases and applications become more sophisticated. Keeping up with the latest developments in algorithms and data structures is essential for professionals in the field.

Ultimately, algorithmic challenges are at the heart of computer science, shaping the way we solve problems, make decisions, and interact with technology. They drive innovation, enable automation, and empower individuals and organizations to tackle complex problems in an ever-changing world.

As technology continues to advance, the role of algorithms and the challenges they present will only become more prominent. Engineers, scientists, and researchers will continue to push the boundaries of what is possible, finding new and creative solutions to the complex problems of our time.

In summary, handling algorithmic challenges is a multifaceted endeavor that requires creativity, analytical thinking, and a deep understanding of algorithms and data structures. From optimizing efficiency to managing large datasets, handling real-time constraints to addressing ethical considerations, these challenges shape the field of computer science and have far-reaching impacts on our society and the way we interact with technology.

Complex problem solving is a skill that is highly valued in many fields and is essential for tackling challenging and multifaceted issues. These problems often involve multiple variables, uncertainties, and interdependencies, making them difficult to solve using simple or straightforward approaches. To successfully navigate complex problems, individuals and teams must employ a variety of strategies and techniques.

One important aspect of complex problem solving is understanding the problem itself. This involves defining the problem, breaking it down into its constituent parts, and identifying the underlying causes and factors. A clear problem definition is the foundation for developing effective solutions.

Gathering information and conducting research are crucial steps in the problem-solving process. This involves collecting data, exploring relevant literature, and consulting experts in the field. In the age of information, access to data and knowledge is easier than ever, and leveraging these resources is essential for informed decision-making.

Another strategy is to employ systems thinking, which involves considering the problem as part of a larger system. This perspective helps individuals understand how various components of the system interact and influence each other. By examining the system holistically, it is possible to identify leverage points for intervention and design more effective solutions.

Developing a structured approach to problem solving is essential for managing complexity. One commonly used framework is the "problem-solving cycle," which consists of stages such as problem identification, solution generation, implementation, and evaluation. Following a systematic process helps ensure that all aspects of the problem are addressed.

Creativity and brainstorming are essential tools in complex problem solving. These techniques encourage individuals to think outside the box, generate innovative ideas, and explore unconventional solutions. Brainstorming sessions with diverse teams can lead to fresh perspectives and breakthroughs.

In some cases, modeling and simulation are used to gain insights into complex systems. Mathematical models and computer simulations allow individuals to experiment with different scenarios, test hypotheses, and visualize the behavior of the system under various conditions. This approach is common in fields like engineering, economics, and environmental science.

Complex problems often involve trade-offs and conflicting objectives. Decision analysis and optimization techniques help individuals weigh the pros and cons of different choices and identify the best course of action. Multi-criteria decision analysis, for example, allows decision-makers to consider multiple criteria simultaneously when evaluating options.

Effective communication is a critical strategy for complex problem solving. It involves conveying ideas, sharing information, and collaborating with others to develop solutions. Clear and open communication is vital when working with multidisciplinary teams or stakeholders with diverse perspectives.

In many cases, experimentation and prototyping are used to test and refine solutions. Prototypes provide a tangible representation of an idea, allowing individuals to identify potential issues and make improvements before full-scale implementation. This approach is common in product development and engineering.

Risk management is another crucial strategy for complex problem solving. Identifying and assessing risks associated with different solutions helps individuals make informed decisions and develop contingency plans. Risk analysis involves considering both the likelihood and impact of potential risks.

In complex problem solving, it's essential to remain flexible and adapt to changing circumstances. Solutions that work in one context may not be suitable for another, and unforeseen challenges may arise. The ability to adjust strategies and pivot when necessary is a valuable skill.

Collaboration and teamwork are often key to solving complex problems. Diverse teams with individuals from different backgrounds and expertise can bring unique perspectives and skills to the table. Working together fosters creativity and collective problem-solving capabilities.

Ethical considerations play a role in complex problem solving as well. It's essential to consider the ethical implications of potential solutions and ensure that they align with values and principles. Ethical decision-making involves weighing the consequences of actions on stakeholders and society as a whole.

Iterative problem solving is a strategy that involves revisiting and refining solutions over time. Complex problems may not have a single "correct" answer, and solutions may need to evolve as new information becomes available. Iterative approaches allow for continuous improvement and adaptation.

In some cases, scenario planning is used to anticipate and prepare for possible future developments. By creating scenarios and exploring different futures, individuals and organizations can better position themselves to respond to changes and uncertainties effectively. Scenario planning is commonly used in strategic planning and risk management.

Finally, complex problem solving requires patience and persistence. Solving intricate problems can be a lengthy and challenging process, and setbacks and failures are part of the journey. Maintaining a positive and determined attitude is essential for staying motivated and finding solutions.

In summary, complex problem solving is a multifaceted process that demands a combination of strategies and approaches. From defining the problem and gathering information to employing systems thinking, creativity, modeling, and decision analysis, individuals and teams must navigate a variety of techniques. Effective communication, risk management, ethics, and adaptability are also crucial aspects of complex problem solving. By employing these strategies and remaining persistent, individuals and organizations can tackle even the most intricate challenges and find innovative solutions.

Chapter 10: Achieving Guru-level Algorithmic Mastery

Mastering algorithmic techniques is a journey that takes individuals from novice to expert in the field of computer science and problem-solving. Algorithmic techniques form the backbone of many computational processes and are vital for solving a wide range of complex problems efficiently and effectively. Whether you're a computer scientist, programmer, data scientist, or engineer, mastering these techniques will empower you to tackle challenges with confidence and creativity.

At the core of algorithmic mastery is a deep understanding of fundamental concepts and principles. You must grasp the building blocks of algorithms, which include data structures, control structures, and basic operations. These foundational elements serve as the raw materials for constructing more complex algorithms.

One critical concept in algorithm design is efficiency. Efficient algorithms are those that can solve a problem quickly and with minimal computational resources. Mastering algorithmic efficiency means knowing how to analyze and compare algorithms in terms of their time and space complexity. You'll learn to choose the most appropriate algorithm for a given problem based on its efficiency characteristics.

Algorithmic problem-solving often involves sorting and searching, which are fundamental techniques. Sorting algorithms arrange a collection of items into a specific order, while searching algorithms locate a particular item within a dataset. You'll explore various sorting and searching algorithms, such as bubble sort, quicksort, binary search, and linear search. Mastering these techniques will enable you to efficiently organize and retrieve data.

Dynamic programming is a powerful problem-solving tool that you'll master on your journey. It involves breaking a complex problem into smaller, overlapping subproblems and solving each subproblem only once, storing the results to avoid redundant computations. Dynamic programming is particularly useful for optimization problems and can significantly improve algorithm efficiency.

Greedy algorithms are another essential technique you'll delve into. These algorithms make a series of locally optimal choices to arrive at a globally optimal solution. You'll learn how to identify problems that can be solved using greedy strategies and how to design and analyze such algorithms.

Graph algorithms are vital for navigating and analyzing complex networks and relationships. As part of your mastery, you'll explore algorithms for traversing graphs, finding shortest paths, and detecting cycles. Graph algorithms are applicable in various domains, from social networks and transportation systems to recommendation engines and network security.

Divide and conquer is a technique that involves breaking a problem into smaller, more manageable subproblems, solving them independently, and then combining their solutions to solve the original problem. Mastering divide and conquer strategies equips you to tackle complex problems efficiently, such as sorting, searching, and finding closest pairs of points.

Data structures are foundational to algorithmic mastery. You'll explore a wide range of data structures, including arrays, linked lists, stacks, queues, trees, and graphs. Understanding when and how to use these data structures is crucial for designing efficient algorithms.

Beyond the basics, you'll dive into advanced algorithmic concepts. These concepts may include advanced data structures like heaps, hash tables, and self-balancing trees. You'll also explore specialized algorithms for specific problem domains, such as geometric algorithms for computational geometry or string algorithms for text processing.

As you progress in mastering algorithmic techniques, you'll encounter algorithmic challenges and complex problems. These challenges will test your problem-solving skills, creativity, and algorithmic expertise. You'll learn to approach problems systematically, apply the appropriate techniques, and optimize your solutions.

Algorithmic challenges come in various forms. Some may require optimizing algorithms for large datasets, while others involve handling real-time data streams. You may encounter optimization problems, where finding the best solution among many alternatives is the goal. Or, you might face combinatorial problems that involve selecting the best combination of elements from a set.

Tackling algorithmic challenges also involves understanding the limitations of computation. You'll delve into computational complexity theory, which categorizes problems based on their inherent difficulty. You'll learn to identify problems that are likely to be intractable and those that can be solved efficiently, as well as how to prove the hardness of problems.

Ethical considerations are an important aspect of algorithmic mastery. You'll explore the ethical implications of algorithmic decisions and learn how to design algorithms that are fair, transparent, and accountable. Understanding the societal impacts of algorithms is crucial in today's world.

Throughout your journey, you'll find opportunities to apply your algorithmic expertise in real-world scenarios. You may work on projects that involve data analysis, machine learning, artificial intelligence, or software development. Mastering algorithmic techniques equips you to excel in these areas and contribute to technological advancements.

As you embark on the path to mastering algorithmic techniques, you'll encounter a diverse and exciting array of challenges. You'll develop problem-solving skills that are not only valuable in computer science but also in various other fields, from engineering to finance to healthcare. Your journey will be characterized by continuous learning, exploration, and a sense of accomplishment as you become proficient in the art and science of algorithms.

Tackling expert-level algorithmic challenges is the culmination of a journey that starts with the basics of computer science and algorithm design. It's a journey that takes you from understanding the fundamentals to mastering advanced techniques, and ultimately, to facing some of the most complex and intricate problems in the field. As you progress in your expertise, you'll encounter challenges that demand not only deep technical knowledge but also creative problem-solving and innovative thinking.

Expert-level algorithmic challenges often involve optimizing algorithms for maximum efficiency and scalability. You'll be asked to develop algorithms that can process large datasets in real-time, minimizing computation time and memory usage. These challenges require a keen understanding of algorithmic complexity and an ability to design algorithms that perform at their best under stringent constraints.

One hallmark of tackling expert-level algorithmic challenges is the need to work with vast and diverse data sources. You may be dealing with terabytes or even petabytes of data, collected from a wide range of sources and formats. Managing and processing such data requires advanced data structures and algorithms to extract meaningful insights efficiently.

In some cases, you'll encounter challenges that involve real-time data streams. These streams can be continuously flowing, and your algorithms must process data as it arrives, making decisions on the fly. Developing algorithms that can handle streaming data and adapt to changing conditions is a specialized skill.

Optimization problems are a common focus in expert-level algorithmic challenges. These problems require you to find the best solution among a vast number of possibilities, often with multiple conflicting objectives. Solving optimization problems efficiently demands advanced optimization techniques, including linear programming, integer programming, and heuristic algorithms.

Combinatorial problems are another category of challenges that experts must tackle. These problems involve selecting the best combination of elements from a set, considering various constraints and criteria. Examples include the traveling salesman problem, which seeks the shortest route to visit a set of cities, and the knapsack problem, which involves selecting items to maximize value within a limited capacity.

In your journey to master expert-level algorithmic challenges, you'll also encounter problems related to data analysis and machine learning. These challenges often involve training complex models on large datasets to make predictions or classifications. You'll need to implement advanced machine learning algorithms, explore deep learning techniques, and optimize model performance.

Parallel and distributed computing become critical as you tackle more significant algorithmic challenges. You'll learn to design algorithms that can harness the power of multiple processors or distributed clusters, enabling faster and more scalable computations. Parallelism and distribution are essential for handling large-scale data processing tasks.

Concurrency and synchronization are essential topics when dealing with complex algorithmic challenges. As you develop algorithms that run concurrently, you'll need to ensure that different parts of the program don't interfere with each other, leading to race conditions or data corruption. Synchronization mechanisms like locks, semaphores, and atomic operations become your tools in managing concurrency.

Memory management and optimization are paramount in expert-level algorithmic challenges. Efficiently utilizing memory resources and minimizing memory leaks become crucial to the performance and stability of your algorithms. You'll delve into advanced memory management techniques, such as manual memory allocation and garbage collection.

Security considerations take on greater importance as you tackle expert-level challenges. You'll learn to design algorithms and systems that are resilient against various security threats, including unauthorized access, data breaches, and denial-of-service attacks. Cybersecurity expertise becomes essential in protecting sensitive data and ensuring the integrity of algorithms.

Ethical considerations continue to be a guiding principle in your journey. As you tackle expert-level algorithmic challenges, you'll be confronted with decisions that have significant ethical implications. You must navigate the balance between technological advancement and ethical responsibility, ensuring that your solutions adhere to ethical principles and societal norms.

Interdisciplinary collaboration becomes more prevalent at the expert level. You may find yourself working with experts from various domains, including domain-specific experts, mathematicians, statisticians, and domain scientists. Collaboration enhances the breadth of knowledge and perspectives available for solving complex problems.

Throughout your journey, you'll encounter algorithmic challenges that push the boundaries of what's possible. These challenges may involve developing algorithms for artificial intelligence, machine learning, natural language processing, or computer vision. You'll be at the forefront of technological innovation, contributing to advancements in fields that impact society and industry.

Innovation and creativity become your allies in tackling expert-level algorithmic challenges. Solutions to these challenges often require thinking outside the box, exploring unconventional approaches, and inventing new techniques. Your ability to innovate and adapt to novel problems will set you apart as an expert in algorithmic problem solving.

As you navigate the world of expert-level algorithmic challenges, you'll continuously refine your problem-solving skills. You'll become adept at breaking down complex problems into manageable subproblems, designing elegant algorithms, and rigorously analyzing their performance. Your expertise will extend beyond solving individual problems to developing a deep understanding of the underlying principles and theories.

Ultimately, mastering expert-level algorithmic challenges is a testament to your dedication, perseverance, and intellectual curiosity. It's a journey that leads to the frontiers of knowledge, where you have the opportunity to shape the future of technology and make a lasting impact on the world. Your mastery of algorithmic techniques equips you to tackle the most demanding and rewarding challenges, contributing to advancements in science, industry, and society as a whole.

BOOK 4
ALGORITHMIC WIZARDRY
UNRAVELING COMPLEXITY FOR EXPERTS

ROB BOTWRIGHT

Chapter 1: The Art of Algorithmic Wizardry

The craft of algorithmic design is a multifaceted discipline that combines art and science to create efficient and elegant solutions to complex problems. At its core, algorithmic design involves the creative process of devising step-by-step procedures to solve specific tasks or address challenges in various domains. The craft of algorithmic design is not limited to computer science; it extends to mathematics, engineering, and many other fields where problems require systematic solutions.

A well-designed algorithm is like a masterfully crafted piece of artwork, characterized by its elegance and efficiency. It captures the essence of problem-solving, distilling it into a series of precise and logical steps. These steps, when executed, yield results that not only solve the problem at hand but also do so in the most efficient and optimal way possible.

The craft of algorithmic design begins with problem analysis. To create an effective algorithm, one must thoroughly understand the problem's requirements, constraints, and objectives. This involves breaking down the problem into its fundamental components and identifying the relationships between them.

Once the problem is understood, the algorithmic designer embarks on the creative process of devising a solution. This often entails brainstorming, sketching out ideas, and exploring different approaches. It's akin to an artist experimenting with various techniques and materials to bring their vision to life.

During the design phase, the algorithmic designer carefully selects data structures and algorithms that will be most suited to the problem. This involves considering factors such as the size of the input data, the desired output, and the computational resources available. The choice of data structures and algorithms is akin to selecting the right tools and materials for a particular artistic project.

Elegance is a hallmark of well-crafted algorithms. An elegant algorithm is one that accomplishes its task with clarity, simplicity, and efficiency. It's akin to a beautiful piece of music or a well-composed painting that conveys its message without unnecessary complexity.

The craft of algorithmic design also requires attention to detail. Every aspect of the algorithm, from the initialization of variables to the termination conditions, must be meticulously considered and implemented. This level of precision ensures that the algorithm operates correctly and reliably.

The iterative nature of algorithmic design is akin to the process of refining an artistic work. Designers often revisit and revise their algorithms, seeking improvements and optimizations. This iterative process involves testing the algorithm with different inputs, analyzing its performance, and making adjustments as needed.

Algorithmic design is not limited to solving a problem once and for all. It involves creating algorithms that are versatile and adaptable to changing circumstances. Just as an artist might create a piece of art that resonates with different audiences, an algorithmic designer aims to develop solutions that can be applied in various contexts.

The craft of algorithmic design also encompasses the art of balancing trade-offs. In many cases, there are competing objectives, such as optimizing for speed while minimizing memory usage. Algorithmic designers must make informed decisions that strike a balance between these conflicting goals.

Documentation is an essential aspect of algorithmic design. Just as an artist may keep a sketchbook or journal to record ideas and insights, algorithmic designers maintain thorough documentation of their algorithms. This documentation serves as a reference for others who may use or build upon the algorithm.

Collaboration is another key element of the craft of algorithmic design. Designers often work in teams, sharing ideas, insights, and expertise to create the best possible solutions. Collaborative efforts can lead to innovative approaches and breakthroughs in algorithmic design.

The craft of algorithmic design also involves a commitment to continuous learning and improvement. Algorithmic designers stay up-to-date with the latest developments in computer science, mathematics, and related fields. They seek inspiration from others in the field and are open to exploring new techniques and technologies.

Real-world applications are where the craft of algorithmic design truly shines. Well-designed algorithms have a tangible impact on society, improving processes in fields ranging from healthcare and finance to transportation and communication. Algorithmic designers take pride in knowing that their work contributes to solving real-world problems and making the world a better place.

The craft of algorithmic design is not limited by boundaries or borders. It transcends cultural and geographical barriers, as algorithms are universal tools that can be applied anywhere in the world. Algorithmic designers from diverse backgrounds bring unique perspectives to problem-solving, enriching the craft with their experiences and insights.

The future of algorithmic design holds endless possibilities. As technology continues to advance, the craft will evolve and adapt to new challenges and opportunities. Algorithmic designers will play a pivotal role in shaping the digital landscape and addressing the complex problems of tomorrow.

In summary, the craft of algorithmic design is a blend of creativity, precision, and problem-solving expertise. It is a discipline that combines the artistry of design with the science of computation. Algorithmic designers are the artists of the digital age, crafting elegant and efficient solutions that have a profound impact on our world.

Mastering algorithmic creativity is a journey that takes you beyond the realm of traditional problem-solving and into the world of innovation and invention. It involves harnessing the power of algorithms not just to find solutions but to generate novel ideas, designs, and concepts. Algorithmic creativity is about pushing the boundaries of what's possible and exploring uncharted territories of innovation.

At its core, algorithmic creativity is the intersection of art and science, where algorithms become tools for the generation of creative content. It's a field that thrives on curiosity, experimentation, and the willingness to break free from conventional thinking. Algorithmic creativity allows you to explore new frontiers in art, music, literature, design, and many other creative domains.

The journey to mastering algorithmic creativity begins with a deep understanding of the creative process itself. You must grasp the psychology of creativity, studying how ideas are formed, how inspiration strikes, and how the mind navigates the creative landscape. This understanding serves as the foundation upon which you'll build your algorithmic approaches to creativity.

One key aspect of algorithmic creativity is the ability to automate creative tasks. This involves developing algorithms that can generate artistic compositions, music compositions, or even literary works. By automating these tasks, you free up your creative energy to focus on refining and enhancing the generated content.

The concept of generative algorithms is central to algorithmic creativity. Generative algorithms are designed to produce new and original content based on predefined rules and parameters. They can mimic the style of a particular artist, generate new melodies, or even create visual art that is indistinguishable from human-created works.

Machine learning and artificial intelligence play a significant role in mastering algorithmic creativity. These technologies enable algorithms to learn from existing creative works and generate new content that aligns with the learned style or genre. For example, a machine learning model can learn the style of a famous painter and then generate new paintings in a similar style.

Experimentation is a fundamental part of algorithmic creativity. You'll explore various algorithmic techniques, tweaking parameters, and trying different approaches to see what yields the most intriguing and innovative results. This iterative process of experimentation and refinement is akin to the artistic process of iteration and revision.

Algorithmic creativity also involves the fusion of different creative domains. For example, you can create algorithms that combine music and visual art, generating multimedia experiences that engage multiple senses simultaneously. The fusion of disciplines can lead to entirely new forms of creative expression.

Constraints are a powerful driver of creativity in algorithmic design. By imposing constraints on algorithms, such as limiting the number of colors in a painting or constraining the melody's rhythm, you can push the algorithm to find innovative solutions within those constraints. Constraints challenge the algorithm to think creatively and find unique ways to express itself.

Human-computer collaboration is a fascinating aspect of algorithmic creativity. Rather than replacing human creativity, algorithms can enhance and amplify it. Artists and creators can collaborate with algorithms, using them as creative tools to explore new possibilities and push the boundaries of their own creativity.

Ethical considerations are essential in the realm of algorithmic creativity. As algorithms generate content that mimics human creations, questions of authorship, plagiarism, and intellectual property rights become complex. Algorithmic creators must navigate these ethical challenges and ensure that their work respects the rights and contributions of human creators.

Algorithmic creativity is not limited to the arts; it extends to problem-solving and innovation in various fields. In engineering and design, for example, algorithms can be used to generate innovative product designs or optimize complex systems. The ability to harness algorithmic creativity for practical innovation is a valuable skill in the modern world.

The world of algorithmic creativity is rich with possibilities for interdisciplinary collaboration. Creators, scientists, engineers, and researchers from diverse backgrounds can come together to explore new frontiers in creativity. Interdisciplinary collaborations can lead to groundbreaking discoveries and innovations that have far-reaching impacts.

Algorithmic creativity also has a playful side. You can create algorithms that generate puzzles, games, or interactive experiences that challenge and engage users in creative ways. Playfulness and exploration are essential aspects of algorithmic creativity, allowing for unexpected and delightful outcomes.

The journey to mastering algorithmic creativity is ongoing. As technology evolves and new algorithms and tools emerge, the possibilities for creative expression and innovation expand. Algorithmic creators must stay curious, open-minded, and adaptable, embracing new technologies and approaches as they continue their creative journey.

In summary, mastering algorithmic creativity is a pursuit that combines the art of imagination with the science of computation. It's a journey that takes you to the cutting edge of creative expression and problem-solving, where algorithms become powerful tools for innovation and invention. As you explore the realms of generative algorithms, machine learning, and interdisciplinary collaboration, you'll unlock new dimensions of creativity that have the potential to shape the future of art, science, and technology.

Chapter 2: Mastering Advanced Algorithmic Paradigms

Advanced algorithmic techniques are the culmination of years of research and innovation in the field of computer science, pushing the boundaries of what's possible in solving complex problems. These techniques represent the cutting edge of algorithm design, enabling us to tackle challenges that were once considered insurmountable. They leverage sophisticated mathematical concepts, advanced data structures, and novel approaches to deliver optimal and efficient solutions.

One of the key pillars of advanced algorithmic techniques is optimization. These algorithms are designed to find the best possible solution among a vast number of potential outcomes. Optimization algorithms are used in various fields, from logistics and finance to engineering and artificial intelligence, to make decisions that maximize or minimize specific objectives.

Dynamic programming is a powerful technique in the realm of advanced algorithms. It breaks down complex problems into smaller, overlapping subproblems and computes their solutions in a bottom-up manner. By storing the solutions to subproblems in a table, dynamic programming algorithms avoid redundant calculations and achieve significant time and space savings.

Advanced algorithmic techniques also delve into the world of approximation algorithms. In situations where finding the exact solution is computationally infeasible, approximation algorithms provide near-optimal solutions that come close to the best possible outcome. These algorithms are indispensable in domains like network design, scheduling, and resource allocation.

Randomized algorithms introduce an element of randomness into algorithm design. They make probabilistic decisions to solve problems efficiently in situations where deterministic algorithms may be impractical. Randomized algorithms are used in areas such as cryptography, data analysis, and optimization.

The study of advanced algorithmic techniques includes graph algorithms, which are fundamental in solving problems related to networks and relationships. Algorithms for finding shortest paths, traversing graphs, and discovering patterns within them play a crucial role in domains like social network analysis, transportation planning, and bioinformatics.

Advanced data structures are the building blocks of many sophisticated algorithms. These data structures, such as balanced trees, heaps, and priority queues, enable efficient data manipulation and retrieval. They are the backbone of algorithms for sorting, searching, and solving complex problems in computational geometry.

In computational geometry, advanced algorithmic techniques are used to solve geometric problems, from finding the convex hull of a set of points to determining the intersection of complex shapes. These algorithms have applications in computer graphics, geographic information systems, and robotics.

Advanced algorithmic techniques also extend into the realm of machine learning and artificial intelligence. Algorithms for clustering, classification, and regression are used to extract meaningful patterns from data and make predictions. These techniques are at the heart of recommendation systems, image recognition, and natural language processing.

The field of quantum algorithms represents the forefront of advanced algorithmic research. Quantum computers leverage the principles of quantum mechanics to perform computations that would be infeasible for classical computers. Quantum algorithms promise breakthroughs in cryptography, optimization, and scientific simulations.

In advanced algorithmic techniques, approximation algorithms provide near-optimal solutions to complex problems. While finding exact solutions can be computationally prohibitive, approximation algorithms offer practical and efficient alternatives. These algorithms are crucial in real-world scenarios where speed and feasibility are paramount.

Bioinformatics is another field where advanced algorithmic techniques shine. Algorithms for sequence alignment, genome assembly, and protein structure prediction enable researchers to unravel the mysteries of genetics and molecular biology. These techniques have far-reaching implications for medicine, drug discovery, and biotechnology.

In network design and optimization, advanced algorithms play a vital role in ensuring efficient resource allocation and connectivity. These algorithms are used in telecommunications, transportation planning, and the design of efficient supply chain networks.

Advanced algorithmic techniques also intersect with the world of game theory. Algorithms for solving games and finding Nash equilibria have applications in economics, auction design, and multi-agent systems.

Quantum algorithms represent a groundbreaking frontier in advanced algorithmic research. Quantum computers harness the principles of quantum mechanics to perform computations that classical computers cannot. These algorithms have the potential to revolutionize cryptography, optimization, and scientific simulations.

In bioinformatics, advanced algorithmic techniques are used to analyze biological data, from DNA sequences to protein structures. These algorithms aid in understanding the genetic basis of diseases, drug discovery, and personalized medicine.

Advanced algorithmic techniques are integral to the development of autonomous systems. Algorithms for path planning, sensor fusion, and decision-making enable self-driving cars, drones, and robotics to navigate and interact with their environments.

In summary, advanced algorithmic techniques represent the pinnacle of computational problem-solving. These techniques leverage optimization, dynamic programming, approximation, randomized algorithms, and advanced data structures to tackle complex challenges across diverse domains. From quantum computing and bioinformatics to artificial intelligence and game theory, advanced algorithms are at the forefront of innovation, driving progress and unlocking new possibilities in science, technology, and society.

The evolution of algorithm design has witnessed several paradigm shifts that have fundamentally transformed the way we approach computational problems. These shifts have been driven by advances in technology, changes in problem domains, and the quest for greater efficiency and scalability. Each paradigm shift has brought new techniques, tools, and perspectives to the field of algorithm design.

One of the earliest paradigm shifts in algorithm design came with the advent of electronic computers. Before computers, algorithms were often expressed in a human-readable form and executed manually. The emergence of electronic computers allowed algorithms to be implemented as machine code, enabling the automation of complex calculations and data processing.

The development of high-level programming languages represented another paradigm shift. High-level languages like Fortran and C allowed programmers to express algorithms in a more natural and abstract manner, freeing them from the intricacies of machine code. This shift democratized algorithm design, making it more accessible to a broader range of individuals and disciplines.

The introduction of algorithmic complexity theory marked a significant paradigm shift in algorithm design. This field provided a rigorous framework for analyzing the efficiency and scalability of algorithms. Algorithms were now evaluated not only in terms of correctness but also in terms of their time and space complexity. This shift led to the development of algorithms that could handle larger datasets and solve more complex problems.

Parallel and distributed computing brought about a paradigm shift in algorithm design, as algorithms needed to be adapted to harness the power of multiple processors or computers. Parallel algorithms aimed to divide tasks into smaller subproblems that could be solved concurrently, improving overall performance. Distributed algorithms addressed challenges of communication and coordination in distributed systems.

The emergence of the internet and the vast amount of data generated online prompted the development of algorithms for data mining and machine learning. This paradigm shift shifted the focus from traditional algorithm design, which often sought exact solutions, to algorithms that could learn patterns and make predictions from data. Machine learning algorithms, such as neural networks and decision trees, opened up new possibilities in fields like image recognition, natural language processing, and recommendation systems.

The rise of big data posed another paradigm shift, as algorithms needed to cope with the challenges of processing and analyzing massive datasets. Distributed computing frameworks like Apache Hadoop and Spark provided the infrastructure for processing large-scale data, while algorithms were adapted to exploit parallelism and distributed resources.

Quantum computing represents a potential future paradigm shift in algorithm design. Quantum algorithms leverage the principles of quantum mechanics to perform computations that would be infeasible for classical computers. These algorithms have the potential to revolutionize cryptography, optimization, and scientific simulations.

The field of algorithmic game theory introduced a new perspective on algorithm design by considering the strategic interactions of rational agents. Algorithms were now designed not only to find optimal solutions but also to address the incentives and strategies of other actors in a game or economic system. This shift has applications in online auctions, ad auctions, and resource allocation in multi-agent systems.

Approximation algorithms offered a paradigm shift for solving optimization problems where finding the exact solution is computationally infeasible. Instead of seeking the optimal solution, these algorithms provide near-optimal solutions that come close to the best possible outcome. This paradigm shift is crucial in real-world scenarios where speed and feasibility are paramount.

In recent years, algorithm design has witnessed a shift toward algorithms for social good. These algorithms aim to address societal challenges, such as healthcare, education, and disaster response. Algorithmic techniques are used to improve access to healthcare, optimize school bus routes, and provide rapid disaster relief.

Ethical considerations have become increasingly important in algorithm design, with a growing awareness of biases and fairness issues in algorithms. This paradigm shift highlights the need to design algorithms that are transparent, accountable, and equitable. Algorithms are now being scrutinized for their impact on privacy, discrimination, and the social fabric.

The field of algorithm design continues to evolve, driven by new challenges and opportunities. The next paradigm shift may come from the intersection of quantum computing, machine learning, and ethical considerations. As algorithms become more integrated into our daily lives, the need for responsible and innovative algorithm design becomes ever more critical.

In summary, paradigm shifts in algorithm design have shaped the evolution of computational problem-solving. From the automation of manual calculations to the development of high-level languages, from algorithmic complexity theory to machine learning and big data, each shift has expanded the possibilities and applications of algorithms. As technology continues to advance, algorithm designers must adapt to new paradigms and embrace the challenges and opportunities they bring.

Chapter 3: Complexity Analysis and Advanced Techniques

The advanced analysis of algorithmic complexity delves deep into understanding the performance characteristics of algorithms, going beyond the basics of time and space complexity analysis. It explores the intricacies of how algorithms behave under various conditions, providing valuable insights for optimizing and fine-tuning algorithmic solutions. Advanced analysis techniques are crucial for addressing real-world challenges where efficiency is paramount.

One important aspect of advanced complexity analysis is the study of worst-case, average-case, and best-case scenarios. While basic complexity analysis often focuses on worst-case scenarios, advanced analysis considers the full spectrum of possible inputs and their associated running times. This nuanced approach provides a more realistic view of algorithm behavior in practice.

Probabilistic analysis is another dimension of advanced complexity analysis. It takes into account the randomness inherent in certain algorithms or input data. By analyzing algorithms' expected performance over probabilistic inputs, we can make informed decisions about their suitability for specific applications.

Amortized analysis is a valuable tool in understanding the long-term performance of data structures and algorithms. It goes beyond per-operation analysis and considers the aggregate cost over a sequence of operations. This perspective helps us identify situations where an algorithm's performance improves over time, even if individual operations may be costly.

Smoothed analysis is a relatively recent addition to advanced complexity analysis. It seeks to bridge the gap between worst-case and average-case analysis by introducing a small amount of random noise to input data. This approach provides a more accurate assessment of algorithm performance under slightly perturbed inputs, which can better reflect real-world scenarios.

Advanced analysis also includes the study of cache complexity, which focuses on how algorithms interact with memory hierarchies, such as caches and main memory. Cache-efficient algorithms aim to minimize data movement between different levels of memory, which is essential for achieving high performance in modern computer systems.

Parallel complexity analysis is crucial in the context of multi-core processors and distributed computing environments. It involves analyzing the efficiency and scalability of algorithms when executed concurrently on multiple processors or machines. Understanding how algorithms can be parallelized and their communication patterns is vital for harnessing the full computational power of modern hardware.

Complexity theory, a fundamental part of advanced analysis, explores the inherent limits of computation. It examines classes of problems and their relationships in terms of computational complexity. Key concepts include P vs. NP, NP-completeness, and the hierarchy of complexity classes, which have far-reaching implications for algorithm design and the feasibility of solving certain problems.

Fine-grained complexity analysis is a relatively recent development in complexity theory. It seeks to classify problems based on their exact computational difficulty, often considering lower bounds on the complexity of specific problems. This area of research has led to insights into the intractability of problems in certain settings and the development of specialized algorithms for practical applications.

Advanced analysis of algorithmic complexity extends to the study of parameterized complexity. It focuses on algorithms whose running time is not solely determined by the input size but also depends on other parameters. Parameterized complexity analysis helps identify tractable cases within seemingly intractable problems.

In distributed computing, advanced complexity analysis considers issues related to fault tolerance, network communication, and consensus algorithms. These aspects are critical in building robust and efficient distributed systems, which are central to modern computing infrastructure.

In computational geometry, advanced analysis explores the efficiency of algorithms for geometric problems. It includes topics like convex hull algorithms, Voronoi diagrams, and geometric data structures, with applications in computer graphics, geographic information systems, and robotics.

The study of advanced algorithmic complexity also encompasses algorithms for online and streaming data. Online algorithms make decisions as data arrives in a stream, often with limited knowledge of future data. Efficient online algorithms are essential in applications like web caching, real-time analytics, and network routing.

Beyond the traditional analysis of worst-case time and space complexity, advanced analysis techniques provide a richer understanding of algorithm behavior. Probabilistic, amortized, smoothed, and cache complexity analyses offer valuable insights into real-world performance. Complexity theory, parameterized complexity, and fine-grained complexity provide a theoretical foundation for understanding the computational limits of algorithms.

In summary, advanced analysis of algorithmic complexity is a multifaceted field that enriches our understanding of algorithms and their behavior. It encompasses a wide range of techniques and perspectives, from probabilistic and amortized analysis to complexity theory and parameterized complexity. These advanced tools are essential for designing algorithms that meet the demands of modern computing, whether in handling big data, optimizing parallel execution, or solving complex computational problems.

Cutting-edge algorithmic approaches represent the forefront of algorithm design, pushing the boundaries of what's possible in solving complex problems. These approaches leverage the latest advancements in computer science, mathematics, and technology to tackle challenges that were once considered intractable. Next, we will explore several cutting-edge algorithmic techniques that are transforming industries and driving innovation.

One of the most exciting developments in algorithm design is the integration of artificial intelligence and machine learning. Machine learning algorithms, such as deep neural networks, have achieved remarkable results in tasks like image recognition, natural language processing, and autonomous decision-making. These algorithms have applications in fields as diverse as healthcare, finance, and autonomous vehicles.

Reinforcement learning, a subfield of machine learning, has gained prominence for its ability to train agents to make decisions through trial and error. This approach has led to breakthroughs in game-playing AI, robotics, and optimization problems. Reinforcement learning algorithms are being used to train robots to perform complex tasks and optimize resource allocation in dynamic environments.

Quantum computing represents a paradigm shift in algorithmic approaches. Quantum algorithms harness the principles of quantum mechanics to perform computations that would be infeasible for classical computers. One of the most famous quantum algorithms is Shor's algorithm, which has the potential to break widely-used encryption schemes. Quantum computing holds promise for solving complex optimization problems, simulating quantum systems, and revolutionizing cryptography.

Blockchain technology has introduced new algorithmic challenges and opportunities. Blockchain algorithms are designed to secure decentralized ledgers and facilitate trustless transactions. Consensus algorithms, like Proof of Work and Proof of Stake, ensure the integrity of blockchain networks. Smart contracts, which are self-executing contracts with the terms of the agreement directly written into code, rely on algorithmic logic to automate transactions.

In the realm of natural language processing, cutting-edge algorithms are transforming how we interact with text and speech. BERT (Bidirectional Encoder Representations from Transformers) and GPT (Generative Pre-trained Transformer) models have revolutionized language understanding and generation. These algorithms power chatbots, virtual assistants, and language translation services.

The field of bioinformatics relies heavily on cutting-edge algorithms to analyze and interpret biological data. Sequence alignment algorithms, such as BLAST, are used to compare DNA and protein sequences, facilitating genetic research and drug discovery. Phylogenetic tree construction algorithms help scientists understand the evolutionary relationships between species.

In computational biology, algorithms for protein folding prediction have the potential to revolutionize drug design and disease understanding. Quantum algorithms are being explored to simulate complex biological processes, providing insights into drug interactions and protein structures.

Optimization algorithms are central to a wide range of applications, from supply chain management to portfolio optimization. Cutting-edge approaches include metaheuristic algorithms like genetic algorithms, simulated annealing, and particle swarm optimization. These algorithms can find near-optimal solutions to complex optimization problems in real-world scenarios.

In the field of computer graphics and computer-aided design, cutting-edge algorithms are essential for creating realistic simulations and 3D modeling. Ray tracing algorithms enable the rendering of photorealistic images and simulations. Real-time rendering techniques, such as rasterization and shading algorithms, power video games and virtual reality experiences.

In robotics, algorithms for motion planning and control are crucial for enabling robots to navigate dynamic environments and interact with objects. SLAM (Simultaneous Localization and Mapping) algorithms allow robots to build maps of their surroundings and determine their own position within those maps. These algorithms are vital for autonomous vehicles, drones, and industrial automation.

Cutting-edge algorithms are also driving advances in healthcare and medical research. Machine learning algorithms can analyze medical images, such as X-rays and MRIs, to assist in diagnosis and treatment planning. Genomic data analysis algorithms help identify genetic markers for diseases and personalize treatment plans.

In finance, algorithmic trading strategies leverage cutting-edge algorithms to make split-second decisions in highly competitive markets. High-frequency trading algorithms use real-time data and sophisticated mathematical models to execute trades at lightning speed. Quantitative finance relies on mathematical algorithms to model financial markets and assess risk.

The Internet of Things (IoT) is powered by algorithms that enable devices to collect, transmit, and analyze data autonomously. Sensor data fusion algorithms merge data from various sensors to provide a comprehensive view of a system. Edge computing algorithms process data locally on IoT devices, reducing latency and conserving bandwidth.

Algorithmic fairness and ethics have become essential considerations in cutting-edge algorithm development. Researchers and practitioners are actively working on algorithms that mitigate bias, promote fairness, and adhere to ethical principles. These efforts are crucial in ensuring that algorithms benefit all members of society without reinforcing existing inequalities.

Quantum machine learning is an emerging field that combines quantum computing with machine learning techniques. Quantum machine learning algorithms promise to solve certain problems exponentially faster than classical counterparts. They have applications in optimization, cryptography, and data analysis.

As we delve into the world of cutting-edge algorithmic approaches, it's important to recognize the profound impact these algorithms have on our daily lives and the industries that shape our society. From artificial intelligence and quantum computing to blockchain technology and bioinformatics, these algorithms are at the forefront of innovation and are poised to continue reshaping the landscape of technology and science.

Chapter 4: Beyond Traditional Sorting and Searching

Innovations in sorting and searching algorithms have been instrumental in improving the efficiency and speed of information retrieval and organization. Sorting algorithms play a fundamental role in computer science and data processing, with applications ranging from databases to scientific simulations. In recent years, researchers and engineers have developed innovative approaches to sorting that leverage modern hardware and parallel processing capabilities.

One such innovation is the development of cache-efficient sorting algorithms. These algorithms aim to minimize data movement between different levels of memory, such as registers, cache, and RAM, which is crucial for achieving high performance in modern computer architectures. Cache-oblivious algorithms, in particular, adapt to the memory hierarchy without explicit knowledge of the cache size or configuration.

Parallel sorting algorithms have also seen significant advancements. In an era of multi-core processors and distributed computing, parallel sorting is essential for efficiently processing large datasets. Innovative algorithms divide the sorting task into smaller subtasks that can be executed concurrently, leveraging the full computational power of modern hardware.

The introduction of sorting networks, such as Bitonic Sort and Batcher's Odd-Even Mergesort, offers highly parallelizable sorting methods. These networks have applications in graphics processing units (GPUs) and other massively parallel architectures.

Another innovation in sorting is the use of hybrid algorithms that combine multiple sorting techniques to optimize performance. For example, Timsort, used in Python's sorting library, combines merge sort and insertion sort to efficiently handle different types of input data.

Searching algorithms have also seen innovations, driven by the need to quickly locate information in vast datasets. Efficient search algorithms are critical for web search engines, database systems, and information retrieval applications.

In-memory databases have led to the development of advanced data structures like B-trees and skip lists that enable fast searching and indexing of data. These data structures strike a balance between storage efficiency and search speed, making them ideal for scenarios where real-time data access is crucial.

Approximate search algorithms are another area of innovation. These algorithms trade accuracy for speed and are well-suited for applications like spell checkers and recommendation systems. They allow for efficient searching in cases where an exact match may not be necessary.

Distributed searching algorithms have become essential in handling the ever-increasing volume of data in distributed systems. Innovations in distributed search focus on achieving high availability and fault tolerance while maintaining low query latency.

Search engines like Elasticsearch and Apache Solr employ distributed indexing and querying techniques to deliver real-time search capabilities across large clusters of machines.

In the context of web search engines, innovations in ranking algorithms have been transformative. PageRank, developed by Larry Page and Sergey Brin at Google, revolutionized how search engines determine the relevance of web pages. Modern search engines use a variety of ranking algorithms, including machine learning-based approaches, to provide users with highly relevant search results.

Searching in natural language has also seen significant innovation. Advancements in natural language processing (NLP) and machine learning have led to the development of sophisticated question-answering systems. These systems can understand and respond to queries in human language, making them valuable in virtual assistants and chatbots.

Fuzzy searching is another innovative approach that allows for searching based on similarity rather than exact matches. This is useful for handling typographical errors, misspellings, and variations in user queries.

In the context of distributed and decentralized systems, innovations in searching have enabled efficient information retrieval in peer-to-peer networks and blockchain-based applications. These algorithms aim to maintain data availability and consistency in a decentralized manner.

Quantum computing presents a unique frontier for innovations in searching. Quantum search algorithms, like Grover's algorithm, offer exponential speedup over classical algorithms for unstructured search tasks. These algorithms have implications for cryptography and database search in a quantum computing era.

In summary, innovations in sorting and searching algorithms continue to drive advancements in computer science and information technology. Cache-efficient sorting, parallel sorting, hybrid sorting, and advanced data structures have improved sorting efficiency. In-memory databases, approximate searching, distributed searching, ranking algorithms, and natural language processing have transformed the landscape of searching. Fuzzy searching, decentralized searching, and quantum search algorithms represent exciting frontiers in this field. As our digital world continues to grow, these innovations will play a crucial role in enabling efficient data organization and retrieval.

Breaking through algorithmic boundaries is a pursuit that has driven computer scientists and engineers for decades. Next, we will explore the relentless quest to overcome limitations and push the frontiers of what algorithms can achieve. One of the primary boundaries that algorithm designers face is computational complexity. Many problems are classified as NP-hard, indicating that finding an exact solution is exponentially time-consuming as the problem size increases. Efforts to break through this boundary have given rise to approximation algorithms, which provide near-optimal solutions in polynomial time. These algorithms are indispensable in fields like logistics, where finding an exact solution for the traveling salesman problem, for instance, becomes impractical as the number of cities grows.

Heuristic algorithms are another approach to tackling NP-hard problems. These algorithms make educated guesses to find solutions quickly and are widely used in fields like artificial intelligence and operations research. For example, genetic algorithms mimic the process of natural selection to evolve better solutions over time.

Quantum computing represents a paradigm shift in breaking through algorithmic boundaries. Quantum algorithms, like Shor's algorithm for factoring large numbers, threaten the cryptographic foundations of the digital world. While quantum computers are still in their infancy, they have the potential to revolutionize fields like materials science, cryptography, and drug discovery.

In the realm of data analytics, the curse of dimensionality has long been a boundary for traditional algorithms. As datasets grow in size and complexity, traditional methods struggle to extract meaningful insights. Dimensionality reduction techniques, such as Principal Component Analysis (PCA) and t-Distributed Stochastic Neighbor Embedding (t-SNE), have emerged to address this challenge.

Deep learning has pushed the boundaries of what is possible in machine learning and artificial intelligence. Deep neural networks, with their many layers, have achieved remarkable results in image recognition, natural language processing, and game playing. These algorithms have transformed industries from healthcare to finance.

In natural language processing, breaking through algorithmic boundaries has meant developing algorithms that can understand and generate human language. Transformer-based models, like BERT and GPT, have demonstrated astonishing capabilities in tasks like language translation, sentiment analysis, and question-answering. These models have revolutionized chatbots, virtual assistants, and content generation.

Reinforcement learning has been pivotal in breaking through boundaries in robotics and autonomous systems. Algorithms like Deep Q-Networks (DQN) and Proximal Policy Optimization (PPO) have enabled robots to learn complex tasks through trial and error. This technology is driving advancements in autonomous vehicles, drones, and industrial automation.

In biology and genetics, algorithms for sequence alignment and protein folding have been critical in understanding the building blocks of life. The Human Genome Project, for instance, relied on innovative algorithms to decode the entire human genome. These breakthroughs have far-reaching implications for personalized medicine and genetic research.

Breaking through algorithmic boundaries in finance has resulted in high-frequency trading algorithms that make split-second decisions in competitive markets. Quantitative finance algorithms use advanced mathematical models to predict market movements and optimize portfolios. These algorithms have reshaped the financial industry and are a testament to the power of algorithmic innovation.

In the world of computer graphics and gaming, real-time rendering algorithms have crossed boundaries by achieving photorealistic graphics. Ray tracing techniques, which simulate the physics of light, create stunning visual effects in video games and movie production. These algorithms have elevated the immersive experience in virtual reality and augmented reality.

Cybersecurity is an ongoing battle to break through the boundaries set by malicious actors. Intrusion detection algorithms continuously evolve to detect new attack patterns and vulnerabilities. Machine learning algorithms analyze network traffic to identify suspicious behavior and potential threats.

Breaking through algorithmic boundaries also includes addressing ethical and fairness concerns. Algorithmic bias and discrimination have been identified as critical challenges in fields like hiring, lending, and criminal justice. Efforts are underway to develop algorithms that promote fairness, transparency, and accountability.

Quantum machine learning is an emerging field that combines quantum computing and machine learning techniques. Quantum machine learning algorithms promise exponential speedup in solving certain problems. They have implications for optimization, cryptography, and data analysis.

The boundaries of algorithmic creativity are continually expanding. Researchers and engineers are driven by curiosity and the desire to solve increasingly complex problems. With the advent of new technologies, such as quantum computing and deep learning, the possibilities for breaking through algorithmic boundaries are more exciting than ever.

In summary, breaking through algorithmic boundaries is a relentless pursuit that drives innovation across various fields. From tackling computational complexity with approximation and heuristic algorithms to leveraging quantum computing and deep learning, the boundaries of what algorithms can achieve continue to expand. These advancements have transformed industries, reshaped the way we interact with technology, and opened up new frontiers for exploration and discovery.

Chapter 5: Dynamic Programming at Expert Levels

Expert-level dynamic programming strategies are the pinnacle of algorithmic problem-solving techniques. These advanced techniques build upon the fundamental principles of dynamic programming and are employed to tackle the most complex and challenging computational problems. Next, we will delve into the intricacies of expert-level dynamic programming and explore the strategies that experts use to optimize their solutions.

One of the key concepts in expert-level dynamic programming is memoization. Memoization involves storing the results of subproblems in a data structure, such as an array or a hash table, to avoid redundant computations. Expert practitioners use memoization to optimize recursive algorithms, significantly reducing their time complexity.

Memoization is especially powerful when dealing with problems that exhibit overlapping subproblems. This means that the same subproblems are encountered multiple times during the computation. By storing and reusing the solutions to these subproblems, experts can dramatically improve the efficiency of their algorithms.

Another advanced technique in dynamic programming is bottom-up or iterative dynamic programming. While the recursive approach is conceptually straightforward, it can lead to stack overflow errors when dealing with a large number of recursive calls. Experts often prefer the bottom-up approach, which starts from the simplest subproblems and iteratively builds up to the desired solution.

To excel in dynamic programming, one must master the art of state transition. State transition involves defining the variables and parameters that represent the current state of the problem. Experts carefully design their state transitions to encapsulate all the information needed to compute the solution incrementally.

In some cases, experts employ optimization techniques, such as space optimization. Space optimization reduces the memory footprint of dynamic programming algorithms. This can be crucial when dealing with problems that have stringent memory constraints.

In addition to memoization and state transition, experts utilize advanced data structures to enhance their dynamic programming solutions. For example, Fenwick trees (also known as binary indexed trees) are employed to efficiently update and query prefix sums, a common operation in many dynamic programming problems.

Expert-level dynamic programming often involves solving complex optimization problems. These problems require not only finding a valid solution but also optimizing it to achieve the best possible outcome. Dynamic programming is a powerful tool for tackling optimization problems, and experts are skilled at formulating and solving them.

Another advanced technique is the use of dynamic programming on trees and graphs. This involves defining dynamic programming states and transitions that capture the recursive nature of tree or graph structures. Experts have a deep understanding of graph algorithms and leverage them to develop efficient dynamic programming solutions.

In competitive programming and algorithmic competitions, speed is of the essence. Experts are known for their ability to implement dynamic programming solutions that run within tight time limits. They optimize their code by avoiding unnecessary computations and leveraging data structures for fast lookups.

Expert-level dynamic programming strategies also encompass problem decomposition. This involves breaking down a complex problem into smaller, more manageable subproblems. Experts excel at identifying the right decomposition strategy that simplifies the problem and leads to an efficient dynamic programming solution.

Some dynamic programming problems involve constraints that experts must carefully consider. These constraints may include limits on time, space, or the number of allowed operations. Experts use their problem-solving skills to devise algorithms that meet these constraints while still delivering accurate results.

Advanced dynamic programming problems often require creative thinking. Experts are not bound by conventional approaches and are willing to explore novel techniques. They draw from a vast arsenal of algorithms and data structures to craft innovative solutions.

In competitive programming, dynamic programming problems can be disguised as other types of problems, such as graph theory or combinatorics. Experts have a keen eye for recognizing the underlying dynamic programming structure hidden within these problems. They apply their knowledge to transform the problem into a dynamic programming challenge.

One of the hallmarks of expert-level dynamic programming is the ability to tackle multi-dimensional and non-standard dynamic programming problems. These problems involve more complex state transitions and often require a deep understanding of the problem domain.

To excel in dynamic programming, experts continuously practice and refine their skills. They participate in coding competitions, solve challenging problems, and study the solutions of other experts. This iterative learning process helps them develop the intuition needed to approach dynamic programming problems effectively.

Expert practitioners of dynamic programming are known for their elegant and efficient solutions. They take pride in crafting code that is not only correct but also concise and easy to understand. Their solutions are a testament to the artistry of algorithmic problem-solving.

In summary, expert-level dynamic programming strategies are the culmination of years of practice, study, and problem-solving experience. Experts employ techniques such as memoization, state transition, bottom-up approaches, and advanced data structures to tackle complex problems efficiently. They excel in problem decomposition, optimization, and creative thinking, making them adept at solving a wide range of dynamic programming challenges. For those aspiring to reach the pinnacle of algorithmic problem-solving, mastering these advanced techniques is essential. Optimizing with dynamic programming is a fundamental technique in algorithmic problem-solving. It involves breaking down complex problems into simpler subproblems and efficiently storing and reusing their solutions to avoid redundant computations. Dynamic programming is especially valuable when dealing with optimization problems where the goal is to find the best solution among many possibilities.

One of the key principles of dynamic programming is the concept of optimal substructure. This means that an optimal solution to a larger problem can be constructed from optimal solutions to its smaller subproblems. By identifying and solving these subproblems systematically, dynamic programming algorithms can find the overall optimal solution.

To optimize with dynamic programming, it is essential to define the state of the problem. The state represents the information needed to compute the solution to a subproblem. For example, in the classic problem of finding the shortest path in a graph, the state might include the current node and the distance traveled so far.

Once the state is defined, the next step is to formulate the recurrence relation. The recurrence relation defines how the solution to a subproblem depends on the solutions to its smaller subproblems. It provides a mathematical equation that expresses the problem's recursive nature.

Dynamic programming solutions can be classified into two main categories: top-down (memoization) and bottom-up (tabulation) approaches. In the top-down approach, also known as memoization, the algorithm starts from the original problem and recursively explores its subproblems. Solutions to subproblems are stored in a data structure, such as an array or a dictionary, to avoid recomputation.

The bottom-up approach, also known as tabulation, starts from the simplest subproblems and iteratively computes solutions for larger subproblems. It builds the solutions in a table-like data structure, typically an array. This approach is often more efficient in terms of both time and space complexity, as it avoids the overhead of recursive function calls.

Dynamic programming algorithms are commonly used to optimize various problems in different domains. For instance, in computer graphics, dynamic programming is employed to optimize the rendering of images and animations. By caching intermediate results, the rendering process becomes faster and more efficient.

In finance, dynamic programming is used to optimize investment portfolios. The goal is to find the best allocation of assets to maximize returns while minimizing risk. Dynamic programming algorithms help investors make informed decisions based on historical data and market conditions.

In natural language processing, dynamic programming is applied to tasks such as text summarization and machine translation. By optimizing the alignment of words and phrases in different languages, these algorithms improve the quality of translations and summaries.

Dynamic programming is also a valuable tool in computational biology. It is used to align DNA sequences, predict protein structures, and analyze genetic data. These applications have far-reaching implications in fields like genomics and drug discovery.

Optimizing with dynamic programming extends beyond traditional computer science and engineering domains. It plays a crucial role in logistics and supply chain management. By finding the optimal routes for deliveries and minimizing transportation costs, dynamic programming algorithms help companies streamline their operations.

In healthcare, dynamic programming is used to optimize treatment plans and resource allocation. For example, in radiation therapy, dynamic programming algorithms optimize the delivery of radiation to minimize damage to healthy tissue while targeting cancer cells.

One of the key advantages of dynamic programming is its versatility. It can be applied to a wide range of problems, from numerical optimization to combinatorial optimization. Whether it's finding the shortest path in a graph, optimizing a manufacturing process, or solving a scheduling problem, dynamic programming provides a systematic approach to optimization.

However, it's essential to recognize that dynamic programming is not a one-size-fits-all solution. Not all problems can be efficiently solved using dynamic programming techniques. Some problems may have too many possible subproblems, making the approach impractical.

Additionally, dynamic programming solutions can be sensitive to problem constraints and input sizes. Optimizing with dynamic programming may require careful consideration of factors such as time complexity, space complexity, and algorithmic complexity.

In some cases, heuristic algorithms or approximation algorithms may be more suitable for optimization. These algorithms provide near-optimal solutions without the computational overhead of exploring all possible subproblems.

While dynamic programming is a powerful technique for optimization, it is not without challenges. Choosing the right state representation and defining the recurrence relation can be non-trivial tasks. Mistakes in these steps can lead to incorrect solutions or inefficient algorithms.

To effectively optimize with dynamic programming, it's essential to practice problem-solving and gain experience with various types of optimization problems. Competitive programming and algorithmic competitions often feature dynamic programming challenges that allow participants to refine their skills.

In summary, optimizing with dynamic programming is a core skill in algorithmic problem-solving. It involves breaking down complex problems, defining states, formulating recurrence relations, and efficiently storing and reusing solutions to subproblems. Dynamic programming is widely used in diverse domains, from computer graphics to finance and healthcare. While it is a powerful technique, it is essential to carefully choose when and how to apply dynamic programming to optimization problems, considering factors like problem constraints and algorithmic complexity. With practice and experience, individuals can become proficient in using dynamic programming to tackle a wide range of optimization challenges.

Chapter 6: Conquering Complex Graph Algorithms

Mastering graph algorithms is crucial in today's world, where complex networks are pervasive. Graphs are versatile data structures that represent relationships between entities, making them essential in various fields, from social networks to transportation systems.

This chapter explores advanced graph algorithms and their applications in handling complex networks. We will delve into techniques that go beyond basic graph traversal and shortest path algorithms, empowering you to tackle intricate real-world problems.

Graph algorithms have become indispensable in analyzing social networks like Facebook and Twitter. These networks consist of millions of interconnected users and provide valuable insights into human behavior, information flow, and online communities.

Advanced graph algorithms enable you to identify influential nodes, discover communities, and detect anomalies in these vast social networks. These insights have practical applications in marketing, recommendation systems, and social media analytics.

Transportation networks, including road networks and airline routes, are other examples of complex graphs. Optimizing routes, minimizing travel times, and ensuring efficient resource allocation are essential tasks in these domains.

Graph algorithms such as Dijkstra's algorithm for shortest paths and the Traveling Salesman Problem solver help streamline transportation systems. They facilitate route planning for GPS navigation, reduce fuel consumption, and improve the overall efficiency of logistics.

In biological research, the analysis of protein-protein interaction networks is critical for understanding cellular processes and diseases. Graph algorithms play a pivotal role in identifying protein complexes, predicting protein functions, and uncovering disease-related genes.

The application of advanced graph algorithms enables scientists to gain insights into intricate biological systems. This knowledge can lead to breakthroughs in drug discovery and personalized medicine, ultimately benefiting human health.

Financial networks, encompassing stock markets and banking systems, rely on graph algorithms to detect fraud and optimize trading strategies. Identifying suspicious transactions and analyzing market trends are vital tasks in this domain.

Graph-based anomaly detection algorithms help detect fraudulent activities by identifying unusual patterns in financial transactions. Additionally, algorithmic trading strategies, such as pairs trading, leverage graph theory to exploit market inefficiencies and generate profits.

In recommendation systems like those used by Amazon and Netflix, graph algorithms are employed to provide personalized recommendations. By analyzing user interactions and product/item relationships, these systems suggest products or content tailored to individual preferences.

Collaborative filtering algorithms, which are based on graph-based user-item interaction graphs, help increase user engagement and drive sales in e-commerce and streaming platforms.

Urban planning and smart city development also benefit from graph algorithms. These algorithms help optimize public transportation networks, reduce traffic congestion, and improve resource allocation in densely populated areas.

Efficient routing and traffic flow optimization are essential for creating sustainable and livable cities. Graph algorithms can help city planners make informed decisions to enhance urban infrastructure and quality of life.

The field of epidemiology relies on graph algorithms for modeling disease spread and mitigating outbreaks. Contact tracing, identifying super-spreaders, and optimizing vaccination strategies are critical tasks in managing epidemics.

Graph-based epidemic models, such as the Susceptible-Infectious-Recovered (SIR) model, allow researchers to simulate disease propagation and evaluate intervention strategies.

In telecommunications, graph algorithms are used to optimize network routing, minimize latency, and ensure high-quality communication services. Efficient data transmission and routing are crucial for maintaining reliable communication systems.

Graph-based routing algorithms, like OSPF and BGP in the Internet's backbone, ensure the efficient flow of data packets, contributing to a seamless online experience.

Environmental monitoring and conservation efforts benefit from graph algorithms as well. Understanding ecological networks, tracking species interactions, and identifying critical habitats are vital for preserving biodiversity.

Graph-based ecological models help ecologists make data-driven decisions to protect endangered species and maintain ecosystem stability.

In the energy sector, optimizing power distribution grids and managing renewable energy sources are pressing challenges. Graph algorithms play a role in improving energy efficiency and sustainability.

Smart grid systems use graph-based algorithms to balance energy supply and demand, reduce power losses, and integrate renewable energy sources into the grid.

The study of citation networks in academia and scientific research relies on graph algorithms for analyzing knowledge dissemination. Identifying influential papers, discovering research trends, and evaluating academic impact are crucial tasks in this field.

Citation networks enable researchers to navigate the vast sea of scientific literature and make informed decisions about their research directions.

As you embark on your journey to mastering graph algorithms, keep in mind that these algorithms are not limited to a single domain. Their versatility allows you to apply them to a wide range of complex networks and solve diverse problems.

To truly excel in this endeavor, it's essential to develop a deep understanding of graph theory, graph representations, and the underlying mathematical principles. Additionally, hands-on experience in implementing and fine-tuning graph algorithms will sharpen your problem-solving skills.

Throughout this book, you will explore advanced graph algorithms, learn how to leverage them in various contexts, and gain insights into their practical applications. By the end of this chapter, you will be equipped with the knowledge and tools to tackle complex networks and extract valuable insights from them.

So, let's dive into the world of mastering graph algorithms for complex networks and unlock the power of graph-based solutions in today's interconnected world.

In the ever-evolving landscape of computer science and data analysis, graph algorithms have emerged as indispensable tools with applications extending far beyond traditional domains. As we delve into the advanced applications of graph algorithms, we'll discover their pivotal role in solving complex problems across various fields.

One of the most prominent applications of graph algorithms lies in the realm of social network analysis. Social networks, such as Facebook, Twitter, and LinkedIn, are vast and dynamic, comprising millions, if not billions, of interconnected users.

Graph algorithms provide the means to analyze these networks, uncovering valuable insights into human behavior, information diffusion, and community structures. Whether it's identifying influential nodes, detecting communities, or tracing the spread of viral content, graph algorithms are at the core of understanding the intricacies of social interactions.

For businesses and marketers, social network analysis powered by graph algorithms can be a game-changer. It enables targeted advertising, recommendation systems, and influencer marketing, allowing companies to reach their audiences more effectively and drive engagement.

In the field of transportation and logistics, graph algorithms play a vital role in optimizing routes and resource allocation. Consider a complex road network or a global airline system, where efficiency is paramount.

Graph algorithms like Dijkstra's algorithm for finding shortest paths and the Traveling Salesman Problem solver help streamline transportation systems. They facilitate route planning for GPS navigation, minimize fuel consumption, and enhance the overall efficiency of supply chains.

Biological research benefits immensely from the application of graph algorithms. One of the primary areas of interest is the analysis of protein-protein interaction networks.

These networks provide insights into cellular processes, protein functions, and disease mechanisms. Graph algorithms help identify protein complexes, predict protein functions, and pinpoint disease-related genes, aiding in drug discovery and personalized medicine.

In finance, the use of graph algorithms is pivotal for detecting fraud and optimizing trading strategies. Financial networks involve vast transaction datasets, making it challenging to identify irregularities or trading patterns manually.

Graph-based anomaly detection algorithms can automatically flag suspicious activities by recognizing unusual patterns within financial transaction graphs. Moreover, algorithmic trading strategies, such as pairs trading, utilize graph theory to exploit market inefficiencies and generate profits.

E-commerce and streaming platforms heavily rely on recommendation systems, and graph algorithms play a significant role in making personalized product or content recommendations. These systems analyze user interactions and product/item relationships within a massive graph of data.

Collaborative filtering algorithms, which leverage graph-based user-item interaction graphs, are instrumental in increasing user engagement and driving sales.

Urban planning and the development of smart cities are also areas where graph algorithms have transformative potential. Optimizing public transportation networks, reducing traffic congestion, and efficiently allocating resources in densely populated areas are key objectives.

Graph algorithms help design optimal routes, minimize congestion, and ensure sustainable urban development.

In epidemiology, the analysis of disease spread and mitigation strategies is vital, especially during pandemics. Graph-based epidemic models, such as the Susceptible-

Infectious-Recovered (SIR) model, simulate the propagation of diseases within populations.

These models allow researchers to predict the impact of interventions, evaluate vaccination strategies, and develop effective containment measures.

Telecommunications companies utilize graph algorithms to optimize network routing, reduce latency, and maintain high-quality communication services. Efficient data transmission and routing are essential for seamless communication in an increasingly connected world.

Graph-based routing algorithms, such as OSPF and BGP, ensure the efficient flow of data packets, contributing to a smooth online experience.

Environmental monitoring and conservation efforts also benefit from graph algorithms. Ecologists use these algorithms to understand ecological networks, track species interactions, and identify critical habitats.

This knowledge aids in the preservation of biodiversity and the protection of endangered species.

The energy sector is undergoing a significant transformation with the integration of renewable energy sources and smart grids. Graph algorithms are instrumental in optimizing power distribution grids, managing renewable energy sources, and reducing energy waste.

Smart grid systems leverage graph-based algorithms to balance energy supply and demand, enhancing sustainability and efficiency.

In academia and scientific research, graph algorithms are employed to study citation networks and analyze knowledge dissemination. Researchers use them to identify influential papers, discover research trends, and evaluate academic impact.

This helps scientists navigate the vast sea of scientific literature and make informed decisions about their research directions.

To excel in the application of graph algorithms across these diverse domains, a deep understanding of graph theory, graph representations, and mathematical principles is essential. Hands-on experience in implementing and fine-tuning these algorithms will sharpen problem-solving skills.

Next, we'll explore advanced graph algorithms and their practical applications, equipping you with the knowledge and tools needed to tackle complex problems in a variety of fields.

So, let's dive into the world of graph algorithms in advanced applications and harness their transformative potential in solving real-world challenges.

Chapter 7: Expert-Level Divide and Conquer Strategies

In the realm of algorithmic problem-solving, Divide and Conquer techniques have long been a cornerstone of efficient solutions. But as we venture into the realm of advanced problem-solving, we'll discover that Divide and Conquer is not a static concept—it evolves and adapts to tackle more complex challenges.

At its core, the Divide and Conquer paradigm is about breaking down a problem into smaller, more manageable subproblems. Each subproblem is then solved independently, and their solutions are combined to solve the original problem.

The power of Divide and Conquer lies in its ability to transform seemingly insurmountable problems into solvable components.

The classic example of this approach is the merge sort algorithm, which divides an array into two halves, recursively sorts each half, and then merges the sorted halves to obtain a fully sorted array.

Merge sort exemplifies the elegance and efficiency of Divide and Conquer algorithms, but the world of advanced problem-solving demands more.

In advanced Divide and Conquer techniques, we encounter problems that require a deeper level of decomposition and creative solutions.

One of the areas where advanced Divide and Conquer techniques shine is in computational geometry. Consider the problem of finding the closest pair of points in a set of points in the plane.

The naive approach would involve comparing every pair of points, resulting in a quadratic time complexity. But through the Divide and Conquer strategy known as the "strip method," we can reduce this to a more efficient linearithmic time complexity.

Here's how it works: we first divide the set of points into two equal halves based on their x-coordinates. We then recursively find the closest pair of points in each half.

However, the crucial step is merging the solutions from both halves while ensuring that we don't miss any potential close pairs.

The "strip method" defines a vertical strip in which no pair of points can have a distance smaller than the smallest distance found in the two halves.

By considering only points within this strip during the merging step, we significantly reduce the number of distance calculations, leading to improved efficiency.

In advanced Divide and Conquer techniques, problem-specific insights like the "strip method" become invaluable.

Another realm where advanced Divide and Conquer techniques are indispensable is in solving optimization problems.

For example, the famous traveling salesman problem (TSP) involves finding the shortest possible route that visits a set of cities and returns to the starting city.

Brute-force solutions for TSP quickly become impractical as the number of cities increases.

However, Divide and Conquer algorithms offer a glimmer of hope. The Held-Karp algorithm is a prime example of an advanced Divide and Conquer approach to TSP.

It decomposes the problem into subproblems, each focusing on finding the shortest route between a subset of cities.

The genius lies in the observation that, to solve the TSP for a set of cities, we must find the shortest route that visits all cities exactly once and returns to the starting city.

This can be accomplished by finding the shortest route for each subset of cities, considering one city as the starting point and one city as the final destination.

By breaking down the problem into these subproblems and carefully combining their solutions, the Held-Karp algorithm provides an optimal solution to the TSP.

Advanced Divide and Conquer techniques are not limited to traditional algorithmic problems. They also find applications in machine learning and data analysis.

For instance, in decision tree-based algorithms like Random Forests, the Divide and Conquer strategy is employed to build a multitude of decision trees, each trained on a different subset of the data.

These individual decision trees are then combined to make predictions, resulting in robust and accurate machine learning models.

Similarly, in parallel computing, Divide and Conquer techniques are vital for optimizing the use of multi-core processors and distributed systems.

Tasks are divided into smaller subtasks that can be executed concurrently, reducing computation time and improving efficiency.

In the world of advanced Divide and Conquer, the devil is often in the details. Algorithm designers must carefully consider how to split problems, how to merge solutions, and how to optimize each step for maximum efficiency.

In many cases, advanced Divide and Conquer algorithms push the boundaries of what is computationally possible, enabling us to tackle problems that were once deemed intractable.

But with this power comes a greater responsibility for algorithm designers to ensure correctness, efficiency, and robustness.

A single misstep in the Divide and Conquer process can lead to incorrect results or inefficient solutions.

As we embark on our journey through advanced Divide and Conquer techniques, we'll explore a multitude of problems that benefit from this strategy, from computational geometry and optimization to machine learning and parallel computing.

With each problem, we'll dissect the Divide and Conquer approach, uncover its intricacies, and learn how to apply it effectively.

In the ever-expanding landscape of algorithmic problem-solving, advanced Divide and Conquer techniques are a powerful tool in our arsenal, enabling us to conquer increasingly complex challenges and push the boundaries of what's possible in computation and data analysis.

So, let's dive deep into the world of advanced Divide and Conquer and unlock its potential to solve the most intricate and demanding problems that the computational world has to offer.

To become a true master of algorithmic problem-solving, one must excel in the art of problem decomposition. This skill is at the heart of breaking down complex problems into manageable components, facilitating elegant and efficient solutions.

Problem decomposition is akin to dissecting a puzzle into its individual pieces, examining each one separately before putting them together to reveal the complete picture.

The essence of decomposition lies in simplifying the problem. By breaking it into smaller, more understandable parts, we gain a clearer understanding of the problem's intricacies.

When faced with a problem, whether it's a coding challenge or a real-world issue, the first step is to analyze and understand it thoroughly. This involves identifying the problem's constraints, requirements, and objectives.

Next, we start the process of decomposition. This often begins with identifying the key components of the problem. For instance, in a software development problem, we might identify modules or functions that need to be implemented.

With the problem components in mind, we can begin breaking them down further into smaller, more manageable subproblems. These subproblems should be well-defined and self-contained, focusing on a specific aspect of the larger problem.

Effective problem decomposition requires a keen sense of abstraction. Abstraction involves simplifying complex concepts or details, emphasizing the essential elements while ignoring unnecessary complexity.

In the realm of computer science and algorithms, abstraction often means representing real-world problems in a way that is amenable to algorithmic solutions.

Consider a common problem in computer graphics: rendering a 3D scene onto a 2D screen. This complex task involves numerous calculations and transformations.

Through problem decomposition and abstraction, we can divide this problem into smaller steps. First, we decompose it into tasks like modeling the 3D scene, determining the camera's perspective, and rendering objects onto the 2D screen.

Each of these tasks can be further abstracted into algorithms. For instance, rendering an object may involve determining its visibility, shading, and placement on the 2D screen.

By breaking the rendering problem into these smaller, more focused components, we can design algorithms to tackle each one individually, leading to a robust and efficient rendering pipeline.

Problem decomposition is not a one-size-fits-all approach; it varies depending on the problem at hand. Different problems may require different levels of decomposition and abstraction.

In some cases, a high-level decomposition may suffice, while in others, a more fine-grained approach is necessary. The key is to strike the right balance that makes the problem more manageable without overcomplicating the solution.

One of the fundamental principles of problem decomposition is modularity. Modularity involves designing components or modules that are self-contained and independent. These modules can be developed, tested, and maintained separately, making the problem-solving process more manageable.

In software engineering, modular design is a cornerstone of building maintainable and scalable systems. By decomposing complex software projects into smaller, reusable modules, developers can work on individual components without disrupting the entire system.

Moreover, modular design fosters collaboration among team members, as each person can focus on a specific module without needing to understand the entire codebase.

To become an expert in problem decomposition, one must also possess a rich toolkit of problem-solving techniques. These techniques include divide and conquer, dynamic programming, and greedy algorithms, among others.

Each of these techniques leverages the power of decomposition to solve problems efficiently.

For instance, divide and conquer involves breaking a problem into smaller subproblems, solving each subproblem independently, and then combining their solutions to solve the original problem.

Dynamic programming, on the other hand, decomposes a problem into overlapping subproblems, solving each subproblem only once and storing its solution for future reference. This technique is especially useful for optimization problems.

Greedy algorithms take a different approach by making a series of locally optimal choices to arrive at a global solution. These choices are often based on the decomposition of the problem into smaller decision points.

Expert problem solvers are adept at selecting the right decomposition strategy and problem-solving technique for each situation.

Moreover, they possess a deep understanding of algorithmic complexity and efficiency. They can analyze the time and space complexity of their solutions, optimizing them for performance and scalability.

Achieving expertise in problem decomposition is not just about solving individual problems; it's about honing a mindset. This mindset involves approaching challenges with a structured, systematic, and analytical approach.

It means seeing the bigger picture while also delving into the details. It requires adaptability, as different problems demand different levels of decomposition and abstraction.

Becoming an expert in problem decomposition is a journey, and like any journey, it takes practice. One must continually challenge themselves with a variety of problems, ranging from simple to complex.

Over time, this practice builds problem-solving intuition—an innate sense of how to approach and break down problems effectively.

Additionally, seeking guidance from experienced problem solvers, studying algorithms and data structures, and participating in coding competitions can all accelerate the development of problem decomposition skills.

In the world of algorithmic problem-solving, the art of problem decomposition is a bridge to expertise. It connects the abstract concepts of algorithms and data structures to real-world problem-solving scenarios.

As you embark on your own journey towards expertise, remember that problem decomposition is a skill that evolves and deepens with experience. It is a skill that opens doors to creative and efficient solutions, enabling you to tackle challenges that once seemed insurmountable.

So, embrace the art of problem decomposition, refine your problem-solving toolkit, and set out to conquer the complex and fascinating problems that await you in the world of computer science and beyond.

Chapter 8: Cutting-Edge Data Structures and Their Applications

Innovations in data structures have played a pivotal role in the evolution of computer science and its applications.

These structures serve as the foundational building blocks for storing, organizing, and manipulating data efficiently.

Over the years, researchers and engineers have continually pushed the boundaries of data structure design, seeking to optimize performance, memory usage, and ease of use.

One of the early innovations in data structures was the creation of arrays and linked lists.

Arrays provide constant-time access to elements, making them suitable for applications where frequent data retrieval is crucial.

Linked lists, on the other hand, allow for dynamic memory allocation and efficient insertion and deletion operations.

Both data structures have found their niches, with arrays used in scenarios where constant-time access is essential and linked lists employed when dynamic memory management is required.

As computing power increased and the need for more complex data structures arose, trees and graphs emerged as fundamental innovations.

Binary trees, in particular, have been widely used for tasks like searching and sorting.

Their hierarchical structure allows for efficient searching, with algorithms like binary search benefiting from their balanced nature.

Balanced binary search trees, such as AVL trees and Red-Black trees, further enhanced data structure efficiency by ensuring logarithmic height and balanced branching.

Graphs, on the other hand, opened up new possibilities for modeling complex relationships and networks.

Innovations like breadth-first search and depth-first search algorithms enabled efficient traversal and analysis of graphs, which are fundamental in various domains, including social networks, transportation, and computer networks.

As the volume and complexity of data grew, so did the need for more advanced data structures.

One of the notable innovations was the introduction of hash tables.

Hash tables combine the efficiency of arrays with the flexibility of linked lists by using a hash function to map keys to array indices.

This allows for constant-time average-case access and is widely used in applications like databases and caches.

The development of advanced hashing techniques, such as open addressing and chaining, further improved hash table performance.

Another significant innovation in data structures was the introduction of self-balancing binary search trees.

These trees automatically maintain balance during insertion and deletion operations, ensuring efficient searching and sorting.

The AVL tree, invented by Adelson-Velsky and Landis, was one of the pioneering self-balancing trees, followed by structures like Red-Black trees and Splay trees.

These innovations made it possible to achieve efficient O(log n) time complexity for operations on sorted data.

In the realm of graph theory, innovations continued with the development of algorithms for finding shortest paths, such as Dijkstra's algorithm and the Bellman-Ford algorithm.

These algorithms have applications in route planning, network routing, and more.

Moreover, innovations like the Floyd-Warshall algorithm enabled finding all-pairs shortest paths efficiently.

The rise of object-oriented programming led to innovations in data structure design, giving birth to abstract data types (ADTs) and data structures that encapsulate both data and behavior.

One of the most famous examples is the dynamic array, which automatically resizes itself as elements are added or removed, providing the benefits of arrays without the need for manual memory management.

Innovations in data structures have also been driven by the demand for efficient data storage and retrieval in databases.

B-trees, for instance, are a self-balancing tree structure optimized for storage systems.

Their ability to maintain balance and handle large datasets makes them essential in database management systems, file systems, and more.

Innovations didn't stop at conventional data structures; they extended into specialized areas like spatial data structures for geographical information systems (GIS).

The R-tree, an innovation in this domain, enables efficient storage and retrieval of spatial data, making it valuable in applications like map databases and location-based services.

The advent of object-oriented programming languages gave rise to innovations like hash maps, which can store objects based on their attributes.

This dynamic mapping of objects to keys has paved the way for highly flexible and expressive data structures.

The evolving landscape of data storage and processing led to innovations in distributed data structures.

Distributed hash tables (DHTs), for example, enable distributed systems to efficiently locate data across a network, supporting applications like peer-to-peer file sharing and content delivery networks (CDNs).

In the era of big data and parallel processing, innovations in data structures extended to parallel and concurrent data structures.

Data structures like concurrent hash maps and lock-free linked lists are designed to support efficient data access and manipulation in multi-threaded and multi-core environments.

These innovations address the challenges of data synchronization and contention, enabling scalable and responsive applications.

In the age of cloud computing, data structures also evolved to meet the demands of distributed and scalable systems.

Distributed data structures, such as distributed caches and distributed queues, play a crucial role in ensuring data consistency and availability in cloud-based applications.

The innovations in data structures have not only transformed the field of computer science but have also had a profound impact on various industries.

From optimizing database management to enabling real-time processing of large datasets, data structures continue to be a driving force behind technological advancements.

Innovations in data structures are an ongoing journey, with researchers and engineers continuously exploring new ways to enhance efficiency, scalability, and versatility. As technology continues to evolve, data structures will remain at the core of computer science, shaping the landscape of computing for years to come.

Advanced data structures play a pivotal role in the efficient handling of complex data and solving real-world problems.

These data structures extend beyond the basics of arrays, linked lists, and binary trees, offering specialized solutions for various application domains.

In practice, the choice of data structure can significantly impact the performance and scalability of software systems.

One such advanced data structure is the Trie, a tree-like structure used to store and retrieve data with keys, often strings, efficiently.

Tries excel in tasks like autocomplete suggestions, spell checking, and IP address storage, where fast prefix matching is essential.

In practice, hash maps are a ubiquitous data structure used to store key-value pairs, offering constant-time average-case lookup and insertion.

Their simplicity and speed make them indispensable in applications like caching, database indexing, and language processing.

In contrast, the Skip List is a versatile structure that combines the simplicity of a linked list with the efficiency of a balanced search tree.

Skip Lists are efficient in maintaining sorted data, supporting both search and insertion in O(log n) time.

They find applications in database indexing and probabilistic data structures.

For applications that require fast range queries and searching, the B-tree is a go-to choice.

B-trees are self-balancing structures that maintain data in sorted order and ensure efficient insertion, deletion, and search operations.

They are commonly used in file systems, databases, and storage systems.

When dealing with hierarchical data, the B+ tree shines.

This tree structure enhances B-trees by keeping data only in leaf nodes, making it optimal for databases and filesystems.

The R-tree is a specialized data structure designed for efficient spatial indexing and querying.

It is essential for applications like geographical information systems (GIS) and map databases, where spatial data must be managed efficiently.

For scenarios requiring fast searching in multidimensional space, KD-trees come into play.

These binary trees partition space in a way that enables efficient range queries and nearest neighbor searches, making them valuable in computer graphics, machine learning, and spatial databases.

In practice, advanced data structures extend beyond the realm of trees and arrays.

The Bloom Filter is a probabilistic data structure used to test whether an element is a member of a set.

While it may have false positives, it offers constant-time membership queries with minimal memory usage, making it suitable for applications like spell checkers and network routers.

Another innovative structure is the HyperLogLog, used for approximate cardinality estimation in large datasets.

It offers highly efficient memory usage while providing reasonably accurate cardinality estimates, making it crucial for big data analytics.

Count-Min Sketch is a data structure used for estimating the frequency of items in a data stream.

It excels in applications like network traffic monitoring and web analytics, where counting occurrences of items in real-time is critical.

In practice, data structures like the Fenwick Tree, also known as a Binary Indexed Tree (BIT), offer efficient solutions for various cumulative data manipulation tasks.

Fenwick Trees are commonly used in scenarios like computing prefix sums and finding the least common ancestor in a tree.

The Quadtree and Octree are spatial data structures used in computer graphics, geographical information systems, and three-dimensional modeling.

They partition space into hierarchical regions to optimize operations like collision detection and spatial indexing.

For efficient text searching, the Suffix Tree and Suffix Array are invaluable.

These structures enable substring searches and pattern matching, making them essential in applications like DNA sequence analysis and natural language processing.

In the world of graphs, advanced data structures like the Union-Find (Disjoint-Set) data structure offer efficient solutions for tasks involving connected components.

They are commonly used in algorithms like Kruskal's algorithm for finding minimum spanning trees.

Graphs also benefit from innovative structures like the Sparse Graph and Compact Graph representations.

These compact data structures save memory and accelerate traversal in large graphs, essential for social networks, recommendation systems, and network analysis.

In practice, advanced data structures are crucial for optimizing memory usage and algorithm performance.

For example, the Bitmask is a simple yet powerful data structure used for efficient storage and manipulation of binary flags.

Bitmasks are prevalent in low-level programming, embedded systems, and computer graphics.

The Interval Tree, or Segment Tree, is a versatile structure used for efficient interval-related queries.

Applications range from scheduling algorithms to geographic information systems.

Red-Black Trees and AVL Trees, though considered basic, are still widely used for maintaining sorted data efficiently.

In practice, their balance properties make them suitable for various applications, such as in-memory databases and compiler symbol tables.

In the realm of distributed systems and concurrency, advanced data structures like Distributed Hash Tables (DHTs) provide efficient key-value storage in decentralized environments.

They are foundational for peer-to-peer networks, content delivery systems, and distributed databases.

The Bloom Filter is also a useful tool for distributed systems, helping reduce network traffic and speeding up data retrieval.

Advanced data structures, including Count-Min Sketch and HyperLogLog, assist in aggregating data from distributed sources in real-time analytics.

In summary, advanced data structures are indispensable tools for solving complex problems and optimizing software performance in real-world applications.

Their versatility and efficiency make them invaluable in a wide range of domains, from databases and networking to artificial intelligence and data analysis.

Understanding when and how to use these structures is essential for building robust and high-performance software systems.

As technology continues to evolve, the development of innovative data structures will remain a critical area of research, driving further improvements in computational efficiency and data management.

Chapter 9: Tackling Algorithmic Puzzles and Enigmas

The art of solving algorithmic puzzles encompasses a wide array of challenges that test one's problem-solving skills and creativity.

These puzzles often require the application of algorithms, data structures, and mathematical concepts to find elegant solutions.

Algorithmic puzzles come in various forms, from traditional pen-and-paper puzzles to coding challenges and competitive programming.

They offer a stimulating way to sharpen one's computational thinking and analytical abilities.

At the heart of algorithmic puzzle-solving is the desire to tackle complex problems using logical reasoning and ingenuity.

These puzzles can be categorized into different types, such as logic puzzles, mathematical puzzles, and combinatorial puzzles.

Logic puzzles involve deducing information from clues to arrive at a solution, like solving Sudoku or the classic Einstein's Riddle.

Mathematical puzzles require applying mathematical principles and formulas to solve problems, like finding the missing number in a sequence.

Combinatorial puzzles involve arranging or selecting elements in a specific way, like solving the Eight Queens Puzzle or the Traveling Salesman Problem.

Algorithmic puzzle-solving is not limited to any specific age group or skill level; it can be enjoyed by beginners and experts alike.

For beginners, algorithmic puzzles serve as an excellent introduction to computational thinking and problem-solving techniques.

They provide a structured way to learn algorithms and data structures while having fun.

As individuals progress in their puzzle-solving journey, they develop a deeper understanding of algorithmic complexities and optimization techniques.

Solving algorithmic puzzles fosters a sense of accomplishment and satisfaction, especially when overcoming challenging hurdles.

It's a journey filled with "Aha!" moments as solutions are unveiled and new strategies are discovered.

Algorithmic puzzles are also an integral part of coding competitions and technical interviews in the tech industry.

Companies use algorithmic puzzles to assess candidates' problem-solving abilities and coding skills.

As such, mastering algorithmic puzzle-solving can open doors to exciting career opportunities in software development and computer science.

Successful puzzle-solving often requires breaking down a complex problem into smaller, manageable subproblems.

This process is known as problem decomposition and abstraction, where the overarching problem is divided into simpler components.

Once the problem is decomposed, individuals can focus on solving each subproblem individually.

This approach allows for a systematic and organized way of tackling complex algorithmic challenges.

Algorithmic puzzles often involve designing and implementing algorithms to achieve a specific goal.

This requires a deep understanding of algorithm design principles and the selection of appropriate data structures.

The efficiency and correctness of the algorithm play a critical role in puzzle-solving success.

Additionally, algorithmic puzzles encourage individuals to think creatively and explore unconventional approaches to problem-solving.

It's not just about finding the "right" answer; it's about finding the most elegant and efficient solution.

Algorithmic puzzle-solving also promotes a growth mindset, where individuals embrace challenges and view failures as opportunities for improvement.

It's a journey of continuous learning and refinement of problem-solving skills.

In competitive programming and coding competitions, participants are often required to solve algorithmic puzzles under time constraints.

This adds an element of urgency and competition, pushing individuals to think on their feet and optimize their solutions for efficiency.

Algorithmic puzzle-solving is not limited to a specific domain or industry; its applications are vast and diverse.

For example, in computer graphics and gaming, algorithms are used to render realistic images and simulate complex environments.

In cryptography, algorithms play a crucial role in securing data and communications.

In artificial intelligence and machine learning, algorithms are used to make predictions and decisions based on data.

Algorithmic puzzle-solving also has real-world applications in optimization problems, such as route planning, resource allocation, and scheduling.

These practical applications demonstrate the relevance of algorithmic puzzle-solving in various fields.

One of the beauties of algorithmic puzzle-solving is its universal appeal.

It transcends language and cultural barriers, making it accessible to a global audience.

Online platforms and communities dedicated to algorithmic puzzles provide a platform for enthusiasts to share their solutions, learn from others, and engage in friendly competition.

These communities foster a sense of camaraderie and collaboration among puzzle enthusiasts.

Moreover, algorithmic puzzle-solving is a lifelong journey.

As individuals continue to explore new puzzles and challenges, they refine their problem-solving skills and deepen their understanding of algorithms and data structures.

The journey is filled with excitement and intellectual curiosity, making it a rewarding pursuit for those passionate about computational thinking.

In summary, the art of solving algorithmic puzzles is a captivating journey that spans various types of puzzles, skill levels, and applications.

It fosters creativity, logical reasoning, and a growth mindset while offering opportunities for learning and career advancement.

Algorithmic puzzle-solving is a universal language that connects individuals worldwide through a shared love for problem-solving and intellectual exploration.

Embarking on the journey of exploring enigmatic algorithmic challenges is akin to setting sail on uncharted waters, where the depths of complexity and innovation beckon.

These challenges often defy conventional problem-solving techniques, pushing the boundaries of computational thinking and algorithmic creativity.

They present tantalizing puzzles that require not only expertise but also a willingness to embrace ambiguity and uncertainty.

Algorithmic challenges come in various forms, from cryptic puzzles that guard their secrets with mathematical rigor to intricate optimization problems that demand elegant solutions.

As we delve into these enigmatic challenges, we encounter a wide spectrum of problem domains and scenarios that test our intellectual prowess.

One of the hallmarks of these challenges is their ability to engage and captivate individuals from diverse backgrounds and skill levels.

For beginners, they serve as a tantalizing glimpse into the world of algorithmic complexity, offering a taste of what lies beyond the basics.

As novices grapple with these enigmas, they gain valuable insights into algorithm design principles, data structures, and algorithmic analysis.

These challenges encourage individuals to think critically, reason logically, and explore unconventional approaches to problem-solving.

The process of deciphering enigmatic algorithmic challenges often involves breaking down complex problems into smaller, more manageable components.

This approach, known as problem decomposition, allows us to tackle intricate puzzles systematically and methodically.

Each subproblem presents an opportunity for discovery and innovation, as we strive to unlock the secrets hidden within.

Algorithmic challenges also teach us the importance of abstraction, where we distill complex problems into simplified models that capture their essential characteristics.

This abstraction enables us to focus on the core issues at hand, providing clarity and insight into the problem-solving process.

The path to unraveling enigmatic algorithmic challenges is fraught with uncertainty and setbacks, but it is through these challenges that we grow and evolve as problem solvers.

The pursuit of a solution may involve numerous iterations, with each attempt bringing us closer to our goal.

These challenges often lead us down unexpected paths, where serendipitous discoveries and "aha" moments illuminate our understanding.

Algorithmic challenges are not confined to the digital realm; they have real-world applications that impact various industries and domains.

In finance, algorithmic challenges play a pivotal role in quantitative trading, risk management, and portfolio optimization.

In healthcare, they aid in medical imaging analysis, drug discovery, and patient care optimization.

In logistics and transportation, algorithmic solutions optimize routes, schedules, and resource allocation.

The enigmatic algorithmic challenges we encounter are not merely intellectual exercises; they have tangible consequences and far-reaching implications.

Algorithmic competitions and hackathons provide platforms for individuals to showcase their problem-solving skills and creativity.

These events foster a spirit of camaraderie and healthy competition, as participants collaborate and pit their wits against one another.

For those seeking career opportunities in technology and computer science, success in algorithmic challenges can open doors to prestigious companies and research institutions.

Companies recognize the value of individuals who can tackle complex problems and devise innovative solutions.

Algorithmic challenges also serve as a proving ground for aspiring data scientists, machine learning engineers, and software developers.

The ability to devise algorithms and optimize them for efficiency is a highly sought-after skill in the tech industry.

As we immerse ourselves in the world of enigmatic algorithmic challenges, we become part of a global community of problem solvers.

Online forums, coding platforms, and open-source projects provide spaces for enthusiasts to collaborate, learn, and share their insights.

These communities transcend geographic boundaries, connecting individuals with a shared passion for algorithmic complexity.

Enigmatic algorithmic challenges invite us to think beyond the boundaries of what is known and explore the uncharted territories of problem-solving.

They require us to approach problems with curiosity, tenacity, and a willingness to embrace the unknown.

Algorithmic challenges also emphasize the importance of continuous learning and self-improvement.

They challenge us to stay updated with the latest developments in algorithms, data structures, and computational techniques.

In the realm of enigmatic algorithmic challenges, there is no shortage of fascinating and unsolved problems waiting to be cracked.

From the enigma of prime numbers to the mysteries of artificial intelligence, the world of algorithmic challenges is a treasure trove of intellectual intrigue.

As we navigate the intricate pathways of these challenges, we gain a deeper appreciation for the beauty and complexity of algorithmic thinking.

Each challenge presents a unique opportunity to hone our skills, expand our horizons, and contribute to the ever-evolving field of computer science.

Algorithmic challenges also encourage us to think about the broader implications of our work.

They prompt us to consider the ethical and societal impact of algorithms and their role in shaping our world.

In summary, exploring enigmatic algorithmic challenges is a journey of intellectual exploration and discovery.

It is a testament to the boundless potential of human ingenuity and the enduring allure of the unknown.

As we delve into the depths of complexity and innovation, we uncover new insights, solve enigmas, and contribute to the ongoing evolution of computer science and technology.

Chapter 10: Unleashing the Full Power of Algorithmic Expertise

Reaching the pinnacle of algorithmic mastery is a journey that demands dedication, perseverance, and a thirst for knowledge. It represents the culmination of years of study, practice, and problem-solving. At this level, algorithmic experts possess a deep understanding of the fundamental principles that underpin computational thinking. They have honed their skills to the point where they can tackle even the most challenging and enigmatic problems with confidence.

Algorithmic mastery is not a destination but a continuous process of growth and refinement. It requires a commitment to lifelong learning and an unwavering passion for the art of algorithm design. Those who reach this pinnacle are not content with mere competence; they strive for excellence in every aspect of their work.

One of the defining characteristics of algorithmic experts is their ability to see beyond the surface of a problem. They possess a keen insight that allows them to identify the underlying patterns and structures that govern complex systems. This ability to abstract and generalize is a hallmark of algorithmic thinking.

Algorithmic mastery is not limited to a specific domain or field; it transcends boundaries and applies to a wide range of disciplines. Whether it's optimizing financial models, solving computational biology problems, or designing cutting-edge machine learning algorithms, experts in the field can adapt their skills to tackle diverse challenges.

At the pinnacle of algorithmic mastery, individuals have a deep appreciation for the elegance and beauty of algorithms. They recognize that simplicity and clarity are often the hallmarks of the most effective solutions. They can distill complex problems into elegant, efficient, and understandable algorithms that stand the test of time.

One of the key principles that algorithmic experts embrace is the idea of algorithmic efficiency. They understand that in the real world, computational resources are finite, and optimization is paramount. Whether it's minimizing time complexity or conserving memory, experts are adept at squeezing every ounce of performance from their algorithms.

Algorithmic experts are also masters of algorithmic analysis. They can rigorously prove the correctness of their algorithms and provide formal guarantees about their performance. This level of rigor is essential when dealing with critical systems and safety-critical applications.

As experts delve deeper into the world of algorithms, they often find themselves pushing the boundaries of what is known. They engage in cutting-edge research, exploring uncharted territory, and seeking solutions to problems that have stumped the best minds in the field. This spirit of innovation and exploration is what drives the field of computer science forward.

At the pinnacle of algorithmic mastery, individuals become mentors and guides for the next generation of algorithmic enthusiasts. They share their knowledge, experience, and wisdom, helping others navigate the complexities of the field. They understand that the true measure of success is not just personal achievement but also the impact they have on the broader community.

Algorithmic experts also recognize the ethical implications of their work. They understand the responsibility that comes with their expertise and strive to use their skills for the betterment of society. They are mindful of the potential biases and ethical dilemmas that can arise when designing algorithms that impact people's lives.

The path to algorithmic mastery is not without its challenges and setbacks. It requires a willingness to embrace failure as a stepping stone to success. Experts understand that every problem they encounter, whether solved or unsolved, is an opportunity for growth and learning.

One of the defining features of algorithmic experts is their ability to collaborate effectively with others. They appreciate the value of diverse perspectives and recognize that solving complex problems often requires a team effort. They are skilled communicators, able to convey their ideas clearly and persuasively to both technical and non-technical audiences.

Algorithmic mastery also involves a deep understanding of data structures. Experts are adept at choosing the right data structures for the task at hand, whether it's a balanced tree for efficient searching or a hash table for rapid lookups. They understand the trade-offs and nuances of different data structures and can make informed decisions about their use.

At this level, experts are also well-versed in the intricacies of algorithmic paradigms. They can identify situations where divide and conquer, dynamic programming, or greedy algorithms are the most appropriate approaches. They can adapt and combine these paradigms to create novel and efficient solutions.

Algorithmic experts are often at the forefront of technological innovation. They are the ones pushing the boundaries of what is possible in fields like artificial intelligence, machine learning, and quantum computing. Their work has the potential to reshape industries and drive the development of transformative technologies.

Reaching the pinnacle of algorithmic mastery is a journey that never truly ends. It is a path marked by continuous learning, exploration, and growth. Those who achieve this level of expertise are not content to rest on their laurels but are driven by an insatiable curiosity and a passion for pushing the boundaries of what is possible.

In summary, the journey to algorithmic mastery is a challenging but rewarding one. It is a path that demands dedication, perseverance, and a commitment to excellence. Those who reach the pinnacle of algorithmic expertise are the ones who shape the future of technology and drive innovation in the field of computer science. Expert-level problem-solving strategies represent the culmination of years of experience and a deep understanding of the principles that govern effective problem-solving. These strategies go beyond simple techniques and embrace a holistic approach to tackling complex challenges. At this level, individuals have honed their problem-solving skills to a razor-sharp edge, and they are capable of addressing a wide range of problems with precision and creativity.

One of the key characteristics of expert-level problem solvers is their ability to deconstruct problems. They have a knack for breaking down complex issues into their constituent parts, allowing them to identify the core elements that need to be addressed. This deconstruction process enables them to approach problems systematically and develop targeted solutions.

Expert problem solvers also excel in pattern recognition. They can quickly identify recurring patterns and structures within problems, drawing upon their extensive knowledge and experience to recognize similarities to previously encountered challenges. This pattern recognition allows them to leverage existing solutions or adapt proven strategies to new situations.

At the expert level, problem solvers possess a deep reservoir of domain-specific knowledge. They have invested time and effort into mastering the intricacies of their chosen field, whether it's mathematics, engineering, computer science, or any other discipline. This domain expertise provides them with a solid foundation upon which to build their problem-solving strategies.

Another hallmark of expert problem solvers is their adaptability. They understand that not all problems can be solved using the same approach, and they are willing to explore different avenues and experiment with various techniques. This flexibility allows them to tailor their problem-solving strategies to the unique characteristics of each challenge they encounter.

Effective communication is a crucial skill for expert problem solvers. They can articulate their thought processes clearly and concisely, both in writing and verbally. This communication prowess enables them to collaborate effectively with others, share their insights, and convey complex ideas in a comprehensible manner.

Expert-level problem solvers are also skilled in critical thinking. They can analyze problems from multiple angles, question assumptions, and identify potential pitfalls or biases in their thinking. This critical approach helps them avoid common cognitive traps and arrive at more accurate and robust solutions.

Collaboration is often a cornerstone of expert problem-solving strategies. Expert problem solvers recognize that they don't have to go it alone and are open to seeking input from others. They understand that diverse perspectives can lead to more innovative and comprehensive solutions.

Mental agility is a hallmark of expert problem solvers. They can quickly switch between different problem-solving modes, whether it's analytical thinking, creative brainstorming, or strategic planning. This adaptability allows them to navigate complex problem-solving landscapes with ease.

Persistence is another key attribute of expert problem solvers. They understand that not all problems are solved overnight and are willing to invest the time and effort required to arrive at a satisfactory solution. They are not discouraged by setbacks or initial failures but view them as opportunities to learn and refine their approach.

Expert problem solvers are also skilled in risk assessment and mitigation. They can evaluate the potential consequences of different courses of action and make informed decisions about the best path forward. This risk management capability ensures that their problem-solving strategies are not only effective but also prudent.

Creativity plays a significant role in expert-level problem-solving strategies. Expert problem solvers are not constrained by conventional thinking and are willing to explore unconventional or innovative approaches. This creative mindset allows them to come up with novel solutions that others may not have considered.

Effective time management is crucial for expert problem solvers. They understand that time is a valuable resource, and they prioritize their efforts based on the importance and urgency of different problems. This time management discipline ensures that they can allocate their energy and attention effectively.

Expert problem solvers are often characterized by their humility. They recognize that there is always more to learn and are open to feedback and self-improvement. They view each problem they encounter as an opportunity for growth and development.

The development of expert-level problem-solving strategies is a journey that requires dedication, continuous learning, and a commitment to excellence. Those who reach this level of expertise are not content with mediocrity but strive for excellence in every aspect of their problem-solving endeavors.

In summary, expert-level problem-solving strategies represent the pinnacle of problem-solving proficiency. They are characterized by a deep understanding of the problem-solving process, adaptability, domain expertise, critical thinking, effective communication, collaboration, mental agility, persistence, risk assessment, creativity, time management, humility, and a commitment to excellence. These strategies enable individuals to tackle complex challenges with precision and creativity, making a significant impact in their chosen fields.

Conclusion

In this comprehensive book bundle titled "ALGORITHMS: COMPUTER SCIENCE UNVEILED," we have embarked on an enlightening journey through the realm of algorithms, from the fundamental principles to the highest levels of expertise. Across the four meticulously crafted volumes, we have explored the intricacies of algorithm design, the analysis of algorithmic complexity, and the art of problem-solving in the digital age.

In "BOOK 1 - COMPUTER SCIENCE: ALGORITHMS UNVEILED," we laid the foundation by introducing algorithmic fundamentals for beginners. We delved into the building blocks of algorithm design, dissected algorithm efficiency and analysis, and embarked on the journey of sorting and searching techniques. This initial volume provided a solid groundwork for readers, equipping them with essential knowledge to navigate the world of algorithms.

"BOOK 2 - MASTERING ALGORITHMS: FROM BASICS TO EXPERT LEVEL" elevated our understanding further, guiding us through the intricacies of algorithmic thinking and introducing advanced sorting and searching algorithms. Dynamic programming and greedy techniques were demystified, while graph algorithms opened up the world of complex networks. This volume equipped readers with the tools to become proficient algorithmic problem solvers.

In "BOOK 3 - ALGORITHMIC MASTERY: A JOURNEY FROM NOVICE TO GURU," our journey continued as we progressed from novice to guru. The divide and conquer strategies provided insights into solving problems efficiently, and we explored advanced data structures and their applications. This volume challenged readers to elevate their skills and embrace algorithmic mastery.

The final installment, "BOOK 4 - ALGORITHMIC WIZARDRY: UNRAVELING COMPLEXITY FOR EXPERTS," pushed the boundaries of algorithmic knowledge. We delved into expert-level techniques, tackled algorithmic puzzles and enigmas, and unleashed the full power of algorithmic expertise. This volume was designed for those who aspire to become true wizards in the field, capable of unraveling even the most complex computational challenges.

As we conclude this journey through "ALGORITHMS: COMPUTER SCIENCE UNVEILED," we hope that readers have not only gained a deep understanding of algorithms but have also developed the problem-solving skills necessary to thrive in the digital age. Whether you are a beginner taking your first steps in computer science or an expert seeking to sharpen your algorithmic prowess, this book bundle has been tailored to meet your needs.

In the ever-evolving world of technology and computer science, the significance of algorithms cannot be overstated. They are the foundation upon which our digital world is built, and mastery of them is a valuable skill that opens doors to innovation and problem-solving. We encourage readers to continue their exploration of algorithms, to apply their newfound knowledge in practical situations, and to contribute to the ever-expanding field of computer science.

Thank you for joining us on this enlightening journey through "ALGORITHMS: COMPUTER SCIENCE UNVEILED." May your algorithmic adventures be filled with curiosity, discovery, and success.

www.ingramcontent.com/pod-product-compliance
Lightning Source LLC
Chambersburg PA
CBHW071233050326
40690CB00011B/2096